Place
a short introduction

Tim Cresswell

Blackwell
Publishing

BLACKWELL PUBLISHING
350 Main Street, Malden, MA 02148-5020, USA
9600 Garsington Road, Oxford OX4 2DQ, UK
550 Swanston Street, Carlton, Victoria 3053, Australia

First published 2004 by Blackwell Publishing Ltd

4   2006

Library of Congress Cataloging-in-Publication Data

Cresswell, Tim.
Place : a short introduction / Tim Cresswell.
   p. cm. – (Short introductions to geography)
Includes bibliographical references and index.
ISBN 1-4051-0671-9 (alk. paper) – ISBN 1-4051-0672-7 (alk. paper)
1. Human geography. 2. Geographical perception. I. Title. II. Series.

GF50.C74 2005
304.2'3–dc22

2003021515

ISBN-13: 978-1-4051-0671-9 (alk. paper) – ISBN-13: 978-1-4051-0672-6 (alk. paper)

A catalogue record for this title is available from the British Library.

Set in 10.5/12pt Palatino
by MHL Production Services, Coventry, United Kingdom
Printed and bound in the United Kingdom
by TJ International Ltd, Padstow, Cornwall

The publisher's policy is to use permanent paper from mills that operate a sustainable forestry policy, and which has been manufactured from pulp processed using acid-free and elementary chlorine-free practices. Furthermore, the publisher ensures that the text paper and cover board used have met acceptable environmental accreditation standards.

For further information on
Blackwell Publishing, visit our website:
www.blackwellpublishing.com

Place

Xd1 .

Short Introductions to Geography are highly accessible books designed to introduce key geographical concepts to students.

For Yi-Fu Tuan

Contents

Figures

Series Editors' Preface

Short Introductions to Geography are highly accessible books, written by leading scholars, that are designed to introduce key geographical ideas to students and other interested readers. Departing from a traditional sub-disciplinary review, they seek to explain and explore central geographical and spatial concepts. These concise introductions convey a sense of the intellectual liveliness, differing perspectives, and key debates that have developed around each concept. Readers are also encouraged to think in new and critical ways about concepts that are core to geographical study. The series serves a vital pedagogic function, encouraging students to recognize how concepts and empirical analyses develop together and in relation to each other. Instructors meanwhile will be assured that students have an essential conceptual reference point, which they can supplement with their own examples and discussion. The short, modular format for the series allows instructors to combine two or more of these texts in a single class, or to use the text across classes with a distinctive sub-disciplinary focus.

Geraldine Pratt
Nicholas Blomley

Acknowledgments

Thinking and writing about place has, for me, been an interactive activity for many years. I have been fortunate enough to have encountered some outstanding teachers as a student. These include Peter Jackson, Jacquie Burgess, Denis Cosgrove, Yi-Fu Tuan and Robert Sack. They have all in inspired me in different ways and I hope some of that inspiration is evident in this book. Now that I am a teacher myself I find myself increasingly indebted to students who have taken ideas and ran with them in startling directions. They are too numerous to mention. I am more particularly indebted to Michael Brown and Carol Jennings for their careful reading of this manuscript and many useful suggestions. Michael Brown is the true inventor of the word anachorism that appears in Chapter Four. Photographs and further inspiration came from Gareth Hoskins and Jo Maddern. Thanks to the following for permission to reproduce copyrighted material. Doreen Massey for the reproduction of her 'Global Sense of Place' paper; Blackwell Publishing for the use of extracts from David Harvey's *Justice, Nature and the Politics of Difference* and The Royal Geographical Society for extracts from Jon May's 'Globalisation and the Politics of Place'. Finally, many thanks to Gerry Pratt and Nick Blomley for the invitation to write this book and to the good people at Blackwell, particularly Angela Cohen, for helping along the way.

1

Defining Place

Human geography is the study of places. It is, of course, many other things but it is, on an intuitive level, a discipline which has place as one of its principle objects of study. Students signing up for geography degrees and courses will often site their interest in different places around the world. Despite this general enthusiasm for the study of places there is very little considered understanding of what the word 'place' means. This is as true in theory and philosophy as it is among the new students signing up for university geography courses. Place is a word that seems to speak for itself.

The popularity of place is an opportunity for geography. It is also a problem as no-one quite knows what they are talking about when they are talking about place. Place is not a specialized piece of academic terminology. It is a word we use daily in the English-speaking world. It is a word wrapped in common sense. In one sense this makes it easier to grasp as it is familiar. In another sense, however, this makes it more slippery as the subject of a book. As we already think we know what it means it is hard to get beyond that common-sense level in order to understand it in a more developed way. Place, then, is both simple (and that is part of its appeal) and complicated. It is the purpose of this book to scrutinise the concept of place and its centrality to both geography and everyday life.

Think of the ways place is used in everyday speech. 'Would you like to come round to my place?' This suggests ownership or some kind of connection between a person and a particular location or building. It also suggests a notion of privacy and belonging. 'My place' is not 'your place' – you and I have different places. 'Brisbane is a nice place.' Here 'place' is referring to a city in a common sense kind of way and the fact that it is nice suggests something of the way it looks and what it is like to be there. 'She put me in my place' refers to more of a sense of position in a social hierarchy. 'A place for everything and everything in its place' is another well-known phrase that suggests that there are particular orderings of things in the world that have a socio-geographical basis. Place is everywhere. This makes it different from other terms in geography like 'territory', which announces itself as a specialized term, or 'landscape' which is not a word that permeates through our everyday encounters. So what is this 'place'?

Cast your mind back to the first time you moved into a particular space – a room in college accommodation is a good example. You are confronted with a particular area of floor space and a certain volume of air. In that room there may be a few rudimentary pieces of furniture such as a bed, a desk, a set of drawers and a cupboard. These are common to all the rooms in the complex. They are not unique and mean nothing to you beyond the provision of certain necessities of student life. Even these bare essentials have a history. A close inspection may reveal that a former owner has inscribed her name on the desk in an idle moment between classes. There on the carpet you notice a stain where someone has spilt some coffee. Some of the paint on the wall is missing. Perhaps someone had used putty to put up a poster. These are the hauntings of past inhabitation. This anonymous space has a history – it meant something to other people. Now what do you do? A common strategy is to make the space say something about you. You add your own possessions, rearrange the furniture within the limits of the space, put your own posters on the wall, arrange a few books purposefully on the desk. Thus space is turned into place. Your place.

40.46ºN 73.58ºW does not mean that much to most people. Some people with a sound knowledge of the globe may be able to tell you what this signifies but to most of us these are just numbers indicating a location – a site without meaning. These co-ordinates mark the location of New York City – somewhere south of Central Park in Manhattan. Immediately many images come into our heads. New York or Manhattan are place names rich with meaning. We might think of skyscrapers, of 9/11, of shopping or of any number of movie locations. Replacing a set of numbers with a name means that we begin to approach 'place'. If we heard that two planes had flown into 40.46ºN 73.58ºW it would not have quite the same impact as hearing that they had flown into New York, into Manhattan, into the Twin Towers. Cruise missiles are programmed with locations and spatial referents. If they could be programmed with 'place' instead, with all the understanding that implies, they might decide to ditch in the desert.

Towards the southern tip of Manhattan and to the east of center is an area – a place – known as the Lower East Side. This is an area which has been known as a place of successive immigrant groups – Irish, Jewish, German, Italian, Eastern European, Haitian, Puerto Rican, Chinese. It is a little to the north of the infamous Five Corners – the setting for the film *The Gangs of New York* (2002). It is a place of closely-knit tenement blocks south of Houston Street – buildings once crammed with large families in small rooms. A succession of moral panics over immigration have focused on this place. It has also been a place of political uprisings and police riots. In the middle of this place is Tompkins Square Park – a little piece of nature in the city built to provide a place of calm in the hurly burly of metropolitan life. It was built in the 1830s and named after the US Vice-President Daniel Tompkins. Later the park became a place of demonstrations by unions and anarchists as well as a place for children and the preaching of temperance. By the 1960s it was the epicenter of a Lower East Side dominated by bohemian counter-cultures, squatters and artists and by the 1980s it was newly respectable – a place where the new cultural elite could savor city life. Needless to say, property prices meant that the buildings were now out of the reach of most people. Homeless people began to sleep in the park. Some of the newly respectable residents were scared by this and supported the removal of homeless people by the police. Once again, in 1986, the park was the site of a demonstration and riot. In the area around the park, from the 1960s on, residents were busy building 84 community gardens in vacant lots. In 1997 Mayor Giuliani transferred responsibility for the gardens from the City Park's Department to the Housing, Preservation and Development Department with the intention that they be sold off for development. The first four gardens were auctioned in July 1997 together with a local community centre. In May 1999, 114 community gardens across New York were saved from development when they were bought by Bette Midler's New York Restoration Fund and Trust for Public Land for a combined total of $4.2 million. However the policy of privatization has continued, and gardens continued to be demolished.

If you visit the Lower East Side now you can dine in any number of fancy and not-so-fancy restaurants, bars and cafes, you can shop in boutiques and admire the brownstone architecture. You can stroll through Tompkins Square Park and visit the remaining community gardens. Crossing over Houston Street to the south you can visit the Lower East Side Tenement Museum in one of the old buildings that formally housed new immigrants. You could, in other words, see many manifestations of 'place'. The museum is an attempt to produce

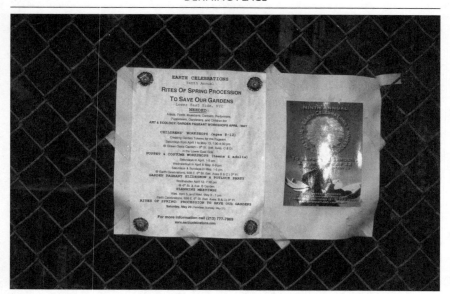

Figure 1.1   *A flyer attached to a community garden fence in the Lower East Side on Manhattan calls for the gardens to be saved from the City government. (Photo by author)*

Figure 1.2   *One of the gardens destroyed by the City Government in New York was Esperanza. People invest a lot in the places they create and were understandably angry at the demolition. (Photo by author)*

a 'place of memory' where the experiences of immigrants will not be forgotten. The gardens are the result of the efforts of immigrants and others to carve out a place from a little piece of Manhattan for their community to enjoy nature. Some of the community gardens – often the first to be leveled – are the sites of *Casitas* – little houses made by the Puerto Rican community to replicate similar buildings from 'home'. They are draped with Puerto Rican flags and other symbols of elsewhere. Old men sit out in the sun watching baseball. Community meetings take place around these eight foot by ten foot buildings. They are, as the urban historian Delores Hayden puts it:

> a conscious choice by community organizers to construct the rural, preindustrial *bohio* … from the island as a new kind of community center in devastated tenement districts such as Lower Harlem, the South Bronx, and the Lower East Side … Painted in coral, turquoise, or lemon yellow, these dwellings recall the colors of the Caribbean and evoke a memory of the homeland for immigrants who find themselves in Alphabet City or Spanish Harlem. (Hayden 1995, 35–6)

Other gardens, ones not planted by Puerto Rican immigrants, are more bucolic, replicating some ideal of an English garden. Yet others are wild nature reserves set aside for local school lessons on biology and ecology. All of these are examples of the ongoing and diverse creation of places – sites of history and identity in the city.

Meanwhile back in Tompkins Square Park there are still tensions between the needs of the homeless to have even the smallest and most insecure 'place-for the night' and the desires of some local residents to have what they see as an attractive and safe place to live and raise families – one that does not include the homeless. Again places are being made, maintained and contested. New York and Manhattan are places. The Lower East Side is a place. The Tenement Museum, community gardens and Tompkins Square Park are all part of the rich tapestry of place making that make up the area in and around 40.46ºN 73.58ºW. We will return to the Lower East Side throughout the book to illustrate the many facets of the use of 'place' in geography.

All over the world people are engaged in place-making activities. Homeowners redecorate, build additions, manicure the lawn. Neighborhood organizations put pressure on people to tidy their yards; city governments legislate for new public buildings to express the spirit of particular places. Nations project themselves to the rest of the world through postage stamps, money, parliament buildings, national stadia, tourist brochures, etc. Within nation-states oppressed

Figure 1.3 *A bucolic scene in a Lower East Side community garden – a place for nature in the city? (Photo by author)*

Figure 1.4 *A casita in a community garden. Note the Puerto Rican flag hanging in the porch and the masks on the wall. Immigrant Puerto Rican groups in New York City place these in their community gardens to recreate something of the place they came from – to make themselves 'feel at home'. (Photo by author)*

groups attempt to assert their own identities. Just as the new student climbs on the bed to put the poster on the wall so the Kosovan Muslim flies a new flag, erects a new monument and redraws the map. Graffiti artists write their tags in flowing script on the walls of the city. This is their place too.

So what links these examples: a child's room, an urban garden, a market town, New York City, Kosovo and the Earth? What makes them all places and not simply a room, a garden, a town, a world city, a new nation and an inhabited planet? One answer is that they are all spaces which people have made meaningful. They are all spaces people are attached to in one way or another. This is the most straightforward and common definition of place – a meaningful location.

The political geographer John Agnew (1987) has outlined three fundamental aspects of place as a 'meaningful location'.

1. Location.
2. Locale.
3. Sense of place.

Perhaps the most obvious point is that all of the places mentioned above are located. They have fixed objective co-ordinates on the Earth's surface (or in the Earth's case a specific location vis-à-vis other planets and the sun). New York is 'here' and Kosovo is 'there'. Given the appropriate scale we could find them on a map. The word place is often used in everyday language to simply refer to location. When we use place as a verb for instance (where should I place this?) we are usually referring to some notion of location – the simple notion of 'where'. But places are not always stationary. A ship, for instance, may become a special kind of place for people who share it on a long voyage, even though its location is constantly changing. By 'locale' Agnew means the material setting for social relations – the actual shape of place within which people conduct their lives as individuals, as men or women, as white or black, straight or gay. It is clear that places almost always have a concrete form. New York is a collection of buildings and roads and public spaces including the community gardens which are themselves material – made of plants and statues and little sheds and houses with fences around them. The child's room has four walls, a window, a door, and a closet. Places then, are material things. Even imaginary places, like Hogwarts School in Harry Potter novels, have an imaginary materiality of rooms, staircases and tunnels that make the novel work. As well as being located and having a material visual form, places must have some relationship to humans and the human capacity to produce and consume meaning. By 'sense of place' Agnew means the subjective and emotional attachment people have to place. Novels and films (at least successful ones) often evoke a sense of place – a feeling that we the reader/viewer know what it is like to 'be there'. We often have a sense of place about where we live, or where we lived when we were children. This is what the author Lucy Lippard has called *The Lure of the Local* (Lippard 1997). It is commonplace in Western societies in the twenty-first Century to bemoan a loss of a sense of place as the forces of globalization have eroded local cultures and produced homogenized global spaces. We will return to this issue of 'placelessness' in Chapter 2.

Agnew's three-part definition of place certainly accounts for most examples of place. In addition, however, it helps to think of place in distinction to two other familiar concepts in human geography – 'space' and 'landscape' – both of which are occasionally substituted with the word 'place'.

Space and Place

An advertisement for a large furniture shop in my Sunday paper read 'Transforming space into place.' Such an advertisement cannot rely on an in-depth understanding of the development of human geography and yet it speaks to one of the central themes in the development of the discipline. The ad suggests that we might want to take the rooms we have recently bought or rented and make them mean something to us by arranging furniture in them – making them comfortable literally and experientially. Humanistic geographers are unlikely to agree that the mere purchase of furniture is going to enact such a transformation but they will recognize the intent.

Space is a more abstract concept than place. When we speak of space we tend to think of outer-space or the spaces of geometry. Spaces have areas and volumes. Places have space between them. Yi-Fu Tuan has likened space to movement and place to pauses – stops along the way.

> What begins as undifferentiated space becomes place as we get to know it better and endow it with value. . . . The ideas 'space' and 'place' require each other for definition. From the security and stability of place we are aware of the openness, freedom, and threat of space, and vice versa. Furthermore, if we think of space as that which allows movement, then place is pause; each pause in movement makes it possible for location to be transformed into place. (Tuan 1977, 6)

Consider the relationship between the sea and land along the coast between Seattle and Vancouver. In his book *Passage to Juneau* (1999) the travel writer Jonathan Raban tells of his trip by boat along that shore. Alongside his travel narrative he tells of the voyage of the explorer Captain Vancouver in his ship HMS Discovery in 1792. Vancouver's task was to map the coast and name it as he went – making it a place of empire. Naming is one of the ways space can be given meaning and become place. Vancouver's journal reports the seemingly nonsensical movements of natives in their canoes in the sea around them. Rather then taking a direct line from point A to point B the natives would take complicated routes that had no apparent logic. To the native canoeists their movements made perfect sense as they read the sea as a set of places associated with particular spirits and particular dangers. While the colonialists looked at the sea and saw blank space, the natives saw place.

> Two world-views were in collision; and the poverty of white accounts of these canoe journeys reflect the colonialists' blindness to the native sea. They didn't get it – couldn't grasp the fact that for Indians the water was a place, and the great bulk of the land was undifferentiated space.
>
> The whites had entered a looking-glass world, where their own most basic terms were reversed. Their whole focus was directed toward the land: its natural harbours, its timber, its likely spots for settlement and agriculture. They travelled everywhere equipped with mental chainsaws and at a glance could strip a hill of its covering forest ... and see there a future of hedges, fields, houses, churches. They viewed the sea as a medium of access to the all-important land.
>
> Substitute 'sea' for 'land' and vice-versa, in that paragraph, and one is very close to the world that emerges from Indian stories, where the forest is the realm of danger, darkness, exile, solitude, and self-extinction, while the sea and its beaches represent safety, light, home, society, and the continuation of life. (Raban 1999, 103)

Raban recounts the visit of the German geographer Aurel Krause while working for the Breman Geographical Society in 1881. He was astonished by what he saw as the local Tlingits' ignorance of their place in the world, which to him was dominated by the enormous mountains that towered behind the small strip of land they inhabited beside the sea.

> In spite of the fact that the Tlingit is constantly surrounded by nature, he is only acquainted with it as it offers him the necessities of life. He knows every bay that lends itself to fishing or the beaching of a canoe ... and for these he has names; but the mountain peaks themselves, even though they are outstanding on account of their shape and size, are scarcely noticed by him. (Raban 1999, 106)

The Tlingits had many names for the sea but the land remained unnamed and seemingly invisible. To the explorers the sea was empty space and the land full of potential places waiting to be mapped and named but this was the mirror image of the Tlinget 'sense of place'.

Space, then, has been seen in distinction to place as a realm without meaning – as a 'fact of life' which, like time, produces the basic co-ordinates for human life. When humans invest meaning in a portion of space and then become attached to it in some way (naming is one such way) it becomes a place. Although this basic dualism of space and place runs through much of human geography since the 1970s it is confused somewhat by the idea of social space – or socially produced space – which, in many ways, plays the same role as place (Lefebvre 1991; Smith 1991).

Place and Landscape

Another concept that frequently appears alongside place in geography texts is landscape. The idea of landscape has a very particular history which dates back to the emergence of mercantile capitalism in Renaissance Venice and Flanders. Landscape painting emerged with the rediscovery of the science of 'optics', new techniques of navigation and the development of a new class of traders. Landscape referred to a portion of the earth's surface that can be viewed from one spot (see Cosgrove 1984; Jackson 1997). It combined a focus on the material topography of a portion of land (that which can be seen) with the notion of vision (the way it is seen). Landscape is an intensely visual idea. In most definitions of landscape the viewer is outside of it. This is the primary way in which it differs from place. Places are very much things to be inside of. Again a literary example illustrates this.

In Raymond Williams' (1960) novel *Border Country* Matthew Price returns to the place of his childhood in the Welsh borders after spending many years at University in England. He is surprised at what he finds when he gets there. He has forgotten the qualities of life that made it a 'place' and replaced it in his mind with a 'landscape'. What follows is an examination of the gap between the idea of the village as 'landscape' and the idea of the village as a lived and felt 'place.' As Matthew realizes he has become an outsider in his own village he reflects on his change of perspective:

> He realized as he watched what had happened in going away. The valley as landscape had been taken, but its work forgotten. The visitor sees beauty,

the inhabitant a place where he works and has his friends. Far away, closing his eyes, he had been seeing this valley, but as the visitor sees it, as the guide book sees it. (Williams 1960, 75)

Later in the novel Matthew gets back into the routine of the village 'It was no longer a landscape or view, but a valley that people were using.' No longer a view from a hill the valley was once again a place. Landscape refers to the shape – the material topography – of a piece of land. This may be apparently natural (though few, if any, parts of the Earth's surface are untouched by humans) landscape or it might be the obviously human, or cultural, landscape of a city. We do not live in landscapes – we look at them.

Place as a Way of Understanding

An important theme of this book is that place is not just a thing in the world but a way of understanding the world. While we hold common-sense ideas of what places are, these are often quite vague when subjected to critical reflection. Most often the designation of place is given to something quite small in scale, but not too small. Neighborhoods, villages, towns and cities are easily referred to as places and these are the kinds of places that most often appear in writing on place. There is little writing on the corner of a favorite room as place at one scale, or on the globe at another. Yet, as Tuan suggested, there is something of place in all of these. So, as it turns out, places as 'things' are quite obscure and hard to grasp.

But place is also a way of seeing, knowing and understanding the world. When we look at the world as a world of places we see different things. We see attachments and connections between people and place. We see worlds of meaning and experience. Sometimes this way of seeing can seem to be an act of resistance against a rationalization of the world, a way of seeing that has more space than place. To think of an area of the world as a rich and complicated interplay of people and the environment – as a place – is to free us from thinking of it as facts and figures. To think of Baghdad as a place is in a different world to thinking of it as a location on which to drop bombs. At other times, however seeing the world through the lens of place leads to reactionary and exclusionary xenophobia, racism and bigotry. 'Our place' is threatened and others have to be excluded. Here 'place' is not so much a quality of things in the world but an aspect of the way we choose to think about it – what we decide to emphasize and what we decide to designate as unimportant. This book is as much about place as a way of knowing as it is about place as a thing in the world. It is as much about epistemology as it is about ontology.

The Remainder of the Book

Space, landscape and place are clearly highly interrelated terms and each definition is contested. The French urban theorist Henri Lefebvre, for instance, has produced a much more sophisticated account of space in which he distinguishes between more abstract kinds of space (absolute space) and lived and meaningful spaces (social space) (Lefebvre 1991). Social space is clearly very close to the definition of place. We will return to debates such as this as we consider the intellectual trajectory of place in geography in the next chapter. For now it suffices to say that the majority of writing about place focuses on the realm of meaning and experience. Place is how we make the world meaningful and the way we experience the world. Place, at a basic level, is space invested with meaning in the context of power. This process of investing space with meaning happens across the globe at all scales and has done throughout human history. It has been one of the central tasks of human geography to make sense of it.

This introduction has provided some provisional outlines of what place means. But this is just a starting point. If it were that easy I could stop now. The fact is that place is a contested concept and what it is that 'place' means is very much the subject of decades of debate in human geography as well as philosophy, planning, architecture and any number of other disciplines. To some in planning, place refers to the built environment. To ecologists, a place is rooted in a distinctive ecology – as a bioregion. To a philosopher, place is a way of being-in-the-world. The rest of this book is an extended investigation of what place means and how the concept has been and might be used by geographers and others.

To that end the remainder of this book is organized as follows. Chapter 2 traces the development of place as a concept since approximately 1950. It shows how place became a central term in North American geography during the late 1970s and early 1980s through the efforts of primarily humanistic geographers (Relph 1976; Tuan 1974a) and traces the roots of this engagement back to the philosophies of meaning – particularly those of Heidegger and Merleau-Ponty. The chapter also traces the appropriation of the term by cultural geography and the linking of place to politics and arguments over who gets to define the meaning of a place (Cresswell

1996). Finally the chapter examines the recent developments in the concept's itinerary such as the notion of increasing 'placelessness' through the effects of 'time-space compression' (Harvey 1989; Augé 1995), Doreen Massey's conception of a 'progressive sense of place' (Massey 1997) and Edward Casey's reinvigoration of a phenomeno-logical view of place and the associated emergence of 'non-representational theory' and the idea of place as practice (Thrift 1997; Casey 1998).

Chapter 3 consists of a critical evaluation of Doreen Massey's paper 'A Global Sense of Place' (Massey 1997). Massey's paper has been widely cited as a plea for a new conceptualization of place as open and hybrid – a product of interconnecting flows – of routes rather then roots. This extroverted notion of place calls into question the whole history of place as a center of meaning connected to a rooted and 'authentic' sense of identity forever challenged by mobility. It also makes a critical intervention into the widely held notions of the erosion of place through globalization and time-space compression. In this chapter her paper (which is included almost in its entirety) is contrasted with a chapter by David Harvey which tackles similar issues in a very different way (Harvey 1996) and a paper by Jon May which mobilizes these understandings in a detailed piece of research into a particular place (May 1996).

Chapter 4 considers empirical examples of ways in which the concept of place has been mobilised in research. The first group of examples concerns the way people have created places. These include the use of place to assert identity in the face of the forces of global processes and movements. We also encounter the way memory and place intersect in the production of heritage places such as museums and how particular visions of place are created in order to get people to live there. But places are not just small and local. Regions and Nations are also places and some geographers have looked at the production of place at a larger scale. These examples reveal how the concept of place can still have salience in the contemporary world in widely divergent contexts. The second set of examples concerns the use of notions of appropriate place to construct normative 'moral geographies' that map particular kinds of people and practice to particular places. Here I draw on my own work on transgression in *In Place/Out of Place* (1996) and work on 'people without place' such as the homeless and refugees as well as how gays, lesbians and bisexuals are made to feel 'out of place'. This work shows how place is used in the construction of ideas about who and what belongs where and when and thus in the construction of those seen as 'deviant' and outside of 'normal' society. While both of these sets of examples concern the connections between place, identity and power they use place in radically different ways and from different political perspectives.

Finally in Chapter 5 I provide an annotated bibliography and lists of key readings and texts, a survey of web resources, pedagogical resources and possible student projects.

2

The Genealogy of Place

Place has always been central to human geography and has been an object of enquiry since at least the First Century AD. The history of geography has taken as one of its central objects the common-sense experienced differences between portions of the Earth's surface. As Carl Sauer wrote in his seminal paper 'The Morphology of Landscape' 'the facts of geography are place facts' (Sauer and Leighly 1963, 321). Or as Richard Hartshorne wrote in *Perspectives on the Nature of Geography* 'The integrations which geography is concerned to analyse are those which vary from place to place' (Hartshorne 1959, 159). A quarter of a century later Allan Pred asserted '[S]ettled places and regions, however arbitrarily defined, are the essence of human geographical inquiry' (Pred 1984, 279). There is probably not much that these three geographers would agree on but they could agree on the importance of place to the subject of geography.

The word 'place' hides many differences. One confusing aspect of the genealogy of place is that place stands for both an object (a thing that geographers and others look at, research and write about) and a way of looking. Looking at the world as a set of places in some way separate from each other is both an act of defining what exists (ontology) and a particular way of seeing and knowing the world (epistemology and metaphysics). Theory is a way of looking at the world and making sense of the confusion of the senses. Different theories of place lead different writers to look at different aspects of the world. In other words place is not simply something to be observed, researched and written about but is itself part of the way we see, research and write. Towards the end of this chapter we will see how geographers and philosophers have sought to show how place is a way-of-being. Here, place is deeply metaphysical and a long way from the simple distinction between one place and another.

The purpose of this chapter is to outline some of the approaches taken to place by geographers (and selected others) through the history of the discipline. Place has also been discussed and used in many other disciplines and walks of life. Architects and urban planners try to evoke senses of place, ecologists and green activists talk of ecological places they call 'bioregions', artists and writers attempt to reconstitute places in their work. As this is a 'short introduction' there is no room to survey all of this literature. The genealogy of place extends well beyond human geography but here we will stick close to the discipline. Some readings and resources from elsewhere are included in the final chapter. The chapter is broadly arranged chronologically to give a sense of the historical progression of an idea. Towards the end however there are many competing definitions of and approaches to place that exist simultaneously. The starting point, however, is regional geography.

Regional Geography

The agreement on the centrality of place to geography between Sauer, Hartshorne and Pred reflects the common-sense notion that geography is a reflection of people's curiosity about the differences between parts of the Earth's surface. It also reflects a history of geography which had seen its practitioners focusing largely on the description of 'regions.' Much of human geography before the 1960s was devoted to specifying and describing the differences between areas of the earth's surface. This 'regional geography' was *ideographic* which is to say that it reveled in the particular. Why was the South of the United States different from the North? How many regions could be identified in England? The central word was region rather than place. The characteristic mode of operation for regional geographers was to describe a place/region in great detail, starting with the bedrock, soil type and climate and ending with 'culture'. A great deal of time was spent differentiating one particular region from others around it – in other words, in drawing boundaries. Some geographers referred to this practice as 'chorology' a spatial version of 'chronology'. While chronology refers to the study of time, chorology refers to the study of regions/places. The origins of chorology date back to the Greek geographer Strabo (First Century AD) who described it as the description of the parts of the earth. The case for geography as chorology has been argued by Richard Hartshorne (Hartshorne 1939).

One influential tradition in human geography was the French tradition of *la géographie humaine* associated with Vidal de la Blache at the end of the nineteenth and beginning of the twentieth century. Although the word place was not its central object its focus on *genre de vie* (ways of life) in particular regions produced work which was remarkable in the way it captured the complicated interplay of the natural and cultural worlds in particular parts of France. *La géographie humaine* succeeded in emphasizing the distinctiveness of particular places in a way which later inspired humanistic geographers (Buttimer 1971; Ley 1977).

Early American cultural geographers also used the term 'region' in their descriptive work on the cultural landscape. In the well known and influential text-book *Readings in Cultural Geography* (Wagner and Mikesell 1962) the editors present what they saw as the main themes in American cultural geography in 1962. The central figure in the text is Carl O. Sauer who had, like de la Blache, rejected the simplistic determinism of the environmental determinists such as Ellen Semple and Ellsworth Huntingdon who had argued that the characteristics of human settlement (culture) were largely a response to environmental imperatives. In other words environment determined society and culture. Rather than seeing culture as determined by the natural environment, Sauer and his followers asserted the importance of culture in transforming the natural environment. In the work of both de la Blache and Sauer culture is given explanatory power. It is no longer simply a result of natural forces. The key themes Wagner and Mikesell identify as central to cultural geography are culture, culture area, cultural landscape, cultural history and cultural ecology. Culture, they argue, rests on a geographical basis in that 'habitual and shared communication is likely to occur only among those who occupy a common area' (Wagner and Mikesell 1962, 3). Cultural geography, therefore, rested of the ranking and classifying of 'culture areas' (these spaces of cultural communication) and an analysis of the ways in which cultural groups affect and change their natural habitats. Again 'place' is not a central concept here but the emphasis on shared cultural spaces suggests the importance of meaning and practice in a given location.

Regional geography was the predominant way of doing geography in Britain during the first half of the century. Approaches ranged from the attempts by Herbertson to show how unique regions emanated from variations in the natural environment (Herbertson 1905) to Fleure's equally ambitious desire to delineate 'human regions' defined by the anthropological particularities of their inhabitants (Fleure 1919 (1996)). In each case the focus was on differentiating one clearly defined region (place) from the next and explaining the logic of the definitions. While Herbertson looked to nature for this logic, Fleure looked to human characteristics.

The importance of regions as places is a theme that still warrants the attention of geographers. Recently, geographers have explored the way regions have been deliberately produced through the activities of formal and informal politics in order to institutionalize particular ideas about government and governance at regional levels. Here the focus is very much on the production of regions rather than the search for regions that already exist (MacLeod and Jones 2001; Paasi 2002). A different argument is made by Nick Entrikin (1985, 1991) as he traces some of the strands of thought in North America which have argued that the stability of democracy is based on an attachment to place and local community. Such 'sectionalism' would, it was hoped, mitigate against 'mass society'. Such views were clearly held by the grandfather of cultural geography Carl Sauer in his defense of traditional ways of life in the face of modern industrialism. To Sauer, an ecologically informed naturalistic philosophy pointed towards the increasing diversity of forms of living, with each community becoming recognizably separate. Activities and forms of human life and culture which threatened regional and place-based distinctiveness were thus a threat. In the conclusion to his book Entrikin suggests that scientific geography – and the fascination with abstract space – had diminished the importance of the particular and that the particular needs to be reclaimed through a narrative understanding of place.

Discovering Place: Humanistic Geography

Given this history and the comments of Sauer, Hartshorne and others it is, as Relph was to remark in 1976 in his book *Place and Placelessness*, surprising that very little attempt had been made to actually define place and distinguish it from its sister concepts of region and area. Place remained a largely common-sense idea. Perhaps the most insistent attempt to come to terms with the concept in the 1960s was made by Fred Lukerman. Echoing the earlier comments of Sauer and Hartshorne, Lukerman had argued that 'Geography is the knowledge of the world as it exists in places' (Lukerman 1964, 167). Lukerman understood places as integrations of nature and culture developing in particular locations with links to other places through the movement of goods and people. This understanding of place is suggestive but also evasive. The words 'culture' and 'nature' are, as Raymond

Williams has reminded us, two of the most complicated words in the English language each of which has many possible meanings (Williams 1985). This definition hardly applies to the corner of a child's room. It also remains unclear how place might be different from area, locality or territory.

Lukerman's interventions aside, the 1970s had not proved promising for the development of a thorough understanding of place. It was largely in this decade that geographers became dissatisfied with geography as an ideographic pursuit. Proper *scientific* disciplines, it was pointed out, liked to generalize and make laws that could be applicable anywhere – not just in Southern California or the South of France. Thus spatial science was born and the concept of region was replaced by the concept of space as a central focus of human geography. The term *space* appeals to the *nomothetic* or generalizing impulse of science. Within spatial science a place was simply a location. Central place theory was the only area in which the term 'place' was often used and here it described locations where particular functions, services and populations were concentrated (Lösch 1954; Christaller and Baskin 1966).

As Arturo Escobar has recently written:

> Since Plato, Western philosophy – often times with the help of theology and physics – has enshrined space as the absolute, unlimited and universal, while banning place to the realm of the particular, the limited, the local and the bound. (Escobar 2001, 143)

Since *the particular* had no place in the hierarchy of values developed in the post-enlightenment world studies of place were often relegated to 'mere description' while space was given the role of developing scientific law-like generalizations. In order to make this work people had to be removed from the scene. Space was not embodied but empty. This empty space could then be used to develop a kind of spatial mathematics – a geometry. But this idea of place as a fascination with the particular and the study of place as 'mere description' depends on a particular naïve view of places as given parts of the human landscape. In the 1970s humanistic geographers began to develop notions of place which were every bit as universal and theoretically ambitious as approaches to space had been.

The development of humanistic geography was, in part, a reaction to the new emphasis on space in spatial science. Central to this enterprise was 'place' which, for the first time, explicitly became the central concept in geographical inquiry. Place, to geographers such as Yi-Fu Tuan (1977; 1974b), Anne Buttimer and David Seamon (1980) and

Edward Relph (1976) was a concept that expressed an attitude to the world the emphasized subjectivity and experience rather than the cool, hard logic of spatial science. But unlike the ongoing traditions of regional and (American) cultural geography, the humanist engagement took a distinctly philosophical turn looking (in what is now a familiar gesture) to continental European philosophy for inspiration. The philosophies of phenomenology and existentialism were central. As we shall see it would be wrong to think of the focus on place as a return to the ideographic concerns with *particular* places that were central to human geography in the first half of the century. Rather place was seen as a universal and transhistorical part of the human condition. It was not so much places (in the world) that interested the humanists but 'place' as an idea, concept and way of being-in-the-world.

The two geographers who have developed this new approach to place most thoroughly are Yi-Fu Tuan and Edward Relph. Yi-Fu Tuan's books *Topophilia* (1974) and *Space and Place* (1977) have had an enormous impact on the history of human geography and, more specifically, the development of the idea of place. Tuan argued that through human perception and experience we get to know the world through places. The term 'topophilia' was developed by Tuan to refer to the 'affective bond between people and place' (Tuan 1974b, 4). This bond, this sense of attachment, is fundamental to the idea of place as a 'field of care'. Tuan defined place through a comparison with space. He develops a sense of space as an open arena of action and movement while place is about stopping and resting and becoming involved. While space is amenable to the abstraction of spatial science and economic rationality, place is amenable to discussions of things such as 'value' and 'belonging.'

This kind of discussion of place is clearly much more than a discussion of location or region. Because place is a product of a 'pause' and a chance of attachment it exists at many scales: 'At one extreme a favorite armchair is a place, at the other extreme the whole earth' (Tuan 1977, 149).

> Place can be as small as the corner of a room or as large as the earth itself: that the earth is our place in the universe is a simple fact of observation to homesick astronauts ... It is obvious that most definitions of place are quite arbitrary. Geographers tend to think of place as having the size of a settlement: the plaza within it may be counted a place, but usually not the individual houses, and certainly not that old rocking chair by the fireplace.
>
> (Tuan 1974a, 245)

Writing in 1974 (before humanistic geography was well known) it is obvious that Tuan was struggling with the abstractions of spatial science. 'Unlike the spatial analyst, who must begin by making simplifying assumptions concerning man, the humanist begins with a deep commitment to the understanding of human nature in all its intricacy' (Tuan 1974a, 246). Spatial science simply missed out too much of the richness of human experience for Tuan and despite the lip service paid to 'place' in definitions to geography no-one was really bothering to figure out what it was. It could not be measured or mapped and laws could not be deduced about or from it.

Edward Relph's approach to place was more explicit in its philosophical commitments to phenomenology. In *Place and Placelessness* (1976) Relph builds on what he describes as our practical knowledge of places – the very everyday and mundane fact of our knowing where to enact out lives. We live in one place, work in another, play football in another. But we are also willing to protect *our* place against those who do not belong and we are frequently nostalgic for places we have left. These human responses, for Relph, reveal the deeper significance of place to human 'being'.

As with Tuan, Relph utilizes the comparison of place with space to make an argument for the significance of place to human life:

> Space is amorphous and intangible and not an entity that can be directly described and analysed. Yet, however we feel or explain space, there is nearly always some associated sense or concept of place. In general it seems that space provides the context for places but derives its meaning from particular places. (Relph 1976, 8)

The continuum which has place at one end and space at the other is simultaneously a continuum linking experience to abstraction. Places are experienced (Tuan's *Space and Place* is subtitled *The Perspective of Experience*).

Relph explicitly builds on the philosophy of Martin Heidegger's work *Being and Time* and particularly the notion of *desien* (approximately 'dwelling'). Desien, for Heidegger was the very essence of existence – the way humans exist in the world. Heidegger used the illustration of a farmhouse in the Black Forest to make his point:

> Here the self-sufficiency of the power to let earth and heaven, divinities and mortals enter in simple oneness into things, ordered the house. It places the farm on the wind sheltered slope looking south, among the meadows close to the spring. It gave it the wide overhanging shingle roof whose proper slope bears up under the burden of snow, and which, reaching deep down, shields the chambers against the storms of the long winter nights. It did not forget the altar corner behind the community table; it made room in its chamber for the hallowed places of childbed and the 'tree of the dead' – for

that is what they called a coffin there; the Totenbaum – and in this way it designed for the different generations under one roof the character of their journey through time. A craft which itself sprung from dwelling, still uses its tools and frames as things, built the farmhouse. (Heidegger 1971, 160)

Place as dwelling, then is a spiritual and philosophical endeavor that unites the natural and human worlds. A properly authentic existence to Heidegger is one rooted in place. If place is broadly analogous to this concept of dwelling then to think of places as simply points on a map or even as 'Toronto' or 'Bombay' is a very shallow conception of place indeed. Note, though, how Heidegger chooses as his example a farmhouse in a forest. It is relatively straightforward to portray such a place as rooted as if in the soil. How this might apply to a modern place in an urban environment is a little harder to imagine. Heidegger's vision is very romantic and nostalgic.

By developing the ideas of Heidegger, Relph sought to escape from simplistic notions of place as location. Relph quoted the philosopher Susanne Langer (also a favourite of Tuan's) noting that place, in the deeper sense, need not have any fixed location at all.

A ship constantly changing its location is nonetheless a selfcontained place, and so is a gypsy camp, an Indian camp, or a circus camp, however often it shifts its geodetic bearings. Literally we say a camp is *in* a place, but culturally it *is* a place. A gypsy camp is a different place from an Indian camp though it may be geographically where the Indian camp used to be.
(Susanne Langer 1953 quoted in Relph, 1976: 29)

Location, then, is not a necessary or sufficient condition of place. Relph works through a list of characteristics of place including their visuality (places have landscapes – we can see them), the sense of community that place supposedly engenders, the sense of time involved in establishing attachment to place and the value of 'rooted-ness' but none of these, he argues, are enough to explain the deeper importance of place to human existence and experience. To get at this Relph returns to phenomenology.

The philosophy of phenomenology was developed by Franz Brentano and Edmund Husserl in the nineteenth century and its central concern is with what philosophers call '*intentionality.*' The word intentionality refers to the 'aboutness' of human conscious-ness. That is to say we cannot (the phenomenologist would argue) be conscious without being *conscious of something.* Consciousness constructs a relation between the self and the world. Relph's argu-ment is that consciousness is not just of something – but something in its place. The only way humans can be humans is to be 'in place.' Place determines our experience.

> The basic meaning of place, its essence, does not therefore come from locations, nor from the trivial functions that places serve, nor from the community that occupies it, nor from superficial or mundane experiences … The essence of place lies in the largely unselfconscious intentionality that defines places as profound centers of human existence.   (Relph 1976: 43)

Essence is a key word here. Phenomenologists saw as one of their principle tasks the discovery of essences. An essence is what makes something what it is. So rather than asking what this place or that place is like, the phenomenological approach to place asks what makes a place a place? What is it that the corner of a child's room shares with an urban garden or Kosovo? Clearly this is not an interest in the particular but a rather grand investigation of a central component of the human world.

At heart this phenomenological enterprise involved the acknowledgment that to be human is to be 'in place.' To the humanist ontological priority was given to the human immersion in place rather than the abstractions of geometric space. As the philosopher of place Edward Casey has put it 'To live is to live locally, and know is first of all to know the place one is in' (Casey 1996, 18). This phenomenological focus on place as experience echoes an earlier observation by Lukerman.

> The study of place is the subject matter of geography because consciousness of place is an immediately apparent part of reality, not a sophisticated thesis; knowledge of place is a simple fact of experience.
>   (Lukerman 1964, 168)

Place is therefore a pre-scientific fact of life – based on the way we experience the world.

The humanistic strand in human geography is a continuous one that informs contemporary debate in many ways. Robert Sack (1992) has written of the connections between place and morality, arguing that in the (post)modern world the primary form our relationship to place takes is often one of consumption. We are sold products in consumption places and they are advertised with reference to a variety of fantastic contexts. The net result of all of this, he argues, is a diminished sense of the consequences of our actions. Morality, to Sack, is based on a knowledge of the consequences of what we do. Consumption, through the disguise of production processes hides the consequences of our purchase and thus creates an amoral consumer's world. A key part of this equation is the spatial scope of such consequences. Hypermodernity is characterized by a characteristic globalism that makes each local action potentially global in its consequences. Its all too much for the individual to process. In the background to Sack's consumer's world lies the alternative of place-based actions where morality is possible due to the close proximity and accountability of the producers of goods. Note how this story of place insinuates the dangerous character of flows and dynamism which disconnect people from place boundedness. This theme, the threat of mobility, is one we shall return to later.

Place as Home?

For many, the most familiar example of place and its significance to people is the idea of home. It is the first example of place in this book. For Tuan, geography is the study of Earth as the home of people (Tuan 1991). By transforming the Earth into home we create places at a myriad of different levels. Tuan argues that the making of places at all scales is seen as the production of a certain kind of homeliness. Home is an exemplary kind of place where people feel a sense of attachment and rootedness. Home, more than anywhere else, is seen as a center of meaning and a field of care. David Seamon (Seamon 1979) has also argued that home is an intimate place of rest where a person can withdraw from the hustle of the world outside and have some degree of control over what happens within a limited space. Home is where you can be yourself. In this sense home acts as a kind of metaphor for place in general.

The centrality of home to humanistic approaches to place owes much to both Heidegger's focus on 'dwelling' as the ideal kind of authentic existence and to the work of another continental phenomenological philosopher – Gaston Bachelard (1994). In Bachelard's book *The Poetics of Space* he considers the house/home as a primal space that acts as a first world or first universe that then frames our understandings of all the spaces outside. The home is an intimate space where experience is particularly intense. To Bachelard the interior arrangement of the house constitutes not one homogeneous place but rather a series of places with their own memories, imaginings and dreams. Thus Bachelard distinguishes between the attic and the basement where the attic is a place of the intellect and rationality and the basement is the place of the unconscious and of nightmares – 'The unconscious cannot be civilized. It takes a candle when it goes to the celler' (Bachelard 1994, 19). To Bachelard, then, the house/home is a particularly privileged kind of place that frames the way people go on to think about the wider universe.

This idea of home as a fundamental place has been questioned by feminists. The feminist geographer Gillian Rose has considered the role of home as place in geography. In her account of humanistic geography (a chapter titled 'No Place for Women') Rose finds much to applaud in the efforts of Tuan, Relph and others. Their willingness to introduce issues of home and the body, for instance, share much with the concerns of feminist geographers. What she finds troubling, however, is the way the idea of place as home is discussed in humanistic geography.

> Although it was often noted that home need not necessarily be a family house, images of the domestic recur in their work as universal, even biological, experiences. Tuan remarked that 'human identification with the familiar, nurturing place has a biological basis'. This enthusiasm for home and for what is associated with the domestic, in the context of the erasure of women from humanistic studies, suggests to me that humanistic geographers are working with a masculinist notion of home/place.
>
> (Rose 1993, 53)

Rose points out that many women do not share the rosy of view of home/place that humanistic geographers place at the center of the discipline. Communities can be stifling and homes can be and often are places of drudgery, abuse and neglect. Many women, Rose argues, would not recognize a view of home/place that is 'conflict-free, caring, nurturing and almost mystically venerated by the humanists' (Rose 1993, 56).

> So, to white feminists who argue that the home was 'the central site of the oppression of women', there seemed little reason to celebrate a sense of belonging to the home, and even less, I would add, to support the humanistic geographers' claim that home provides the ultimate sense of place.   (Rose 1993, 55)

While humanists claim that place is a universal experience (while at the same time using the word 'man' as the universal person) they fail to recognize the differences between people and their relation to place. In the search for 'essence' – 'difference' has no place.

Not all feminists share Rose's view although most would share her suspicion of the idea of home as always warm and caring. The black feminist author bell hooks has written of home as a place of resistance (hooks 1990; Young, I.M. 1997). As a black child growing up in a starkly segregated society hooks experienced her home as a place of care and relative freedom from the oppression black people suffered in the world outside and, especially, in the homes of white people where they worked as domestic servants. To hooks, home and the activities that go into making home can have significance as forms of resistance in an oppressive white world. Home may indeed act as a particular kind of safe place where (some) people are relatively free to forge their own identities. For hooks, homeplace is an empowering place.

Radical Human Geography and the Politics of Place

Discussions of place as home begin to reveal some of the political issues that surround place. While the geographical engagement with phenomenological enquiry rescued the notion of place from oblivion it simultaneously constructed a notion of place which some see as essentialist and exclusionary, based on notions of rooted authenticity that are increasingly unsustainable in the (post)modern world. Heidegger, just like de la Blache and Sauer, tended to focus on rural images and places in order to make their arguments about regions and place. At the beginning of the twenty-first century it is very hard to see how these observations can be applied even to modern rurality let alone the modern metropolis. This has led geographers informed by Marxism, feminism and post-structuralism to shy away from place as a concept. When they have engaged with place it has been in a critical mode – pointing out how places are socially constructed and how these constructions are founded on acts of exclusion.

David Harvey, for instance, has recently argued that the significance of place has increased under the conditions of flexible accumulation, postmodernity and time-space compression (Harvey 1996). He suggests this because, as he sees it, places are under all kinds of threats from variously; the restructuring of economic spatial relations at a global level, the increased mobility of production, capital, merchanting and marketing and the increasing need to differentiate between places in order to compete. Place, in Harvey's lexicon, is a form of fixed capital which exists in tension with other forms of mobile capital. The tension between the fixed and the mobile produces cycles of place investment and disinvestment which contributes to an unstable process of uneven development across the globe. In the story that Harvey tells, place has a more ambivalent role than in the celebrations of humanism. Place is certainly threatened by the hypermobility of flexible capital, mass communications and transportation. Political struggles over place, therefore, often provide opportunities for resistance to the mobile forces of capitalism. But struggles for place identity also appeal to the parochial and exclusive forces of bigotry and nationalism. The identification of place usually involves an us/them distinction in which the other is devalued (see Chapter 4 for an extended discussion of this theme).

Around the late 1980s geographers began to seriously engage with the wider fields of social theory and cultural studies. The distinction between so-called humanistic geographers on the one hand and radical geographers on the other began to break down and a new cultural geography informed by Raymond Williams, Antonio Gramsci and the work of the Birmingham school of Cultural Studies emerged. On both sides of the Atlantic geographers began to confidently assert the importance of geography to critical theory. Class, gender, and race have so often been treated as if they happened on the head of a pin. Well they don't – they happen in space and place. By taking space and place seriously, it was argued, we can provide another tool to demystify and understand the forces that effect and manipulate our everyday lives.

It was in this context that I wrote *In Place/Out of Place* (Cresswell 1996). In this book I argued that people, things and practices were often strongly linked to particular places and that when this link was broken – when people acted 'out of place' – they were deemed to have committed a 'transgression'. I used the examples of graffiti artists in New York City, the peace campers of Greenham Common (UK) and new age travellers in the British countryside. In each case people and practices were considered (by the media, government, etc.) to have transgressed the supposedly common-sense link between place and the things that go on it. The purpose of this work was to show how place does not have meanings that are natural and obvious but ones that are created by some people with more power than others to define what is and is not appropriate. It also showed how people are able to resist the construction of expectations about practice through place by using places and their established meanings in subversive ways. Throughout issues of age, gender, class, lifestyle, sexuality and ethnicity were at the fore. All of these had been largely ignored by traditions such as regional geography and humanistic geography. We will return to these themes of exclusion and transgression in Chapter 4.

Critical cultural geographers began to use place in a myriad of ways which revealed the complicated connections between place, meaning and power. Benjamin Forest, for instance, considered how the gay population of West Hollywood in California successfully mobilized symbols of gay identity such as creativity and progressive politics during the campaign to incorporate West Hollywood in 1984 (Forest 1995). He argued that having a politically constituted place as a geographical focus of gay identity allowed the gay community to construct an identity based on more than sexual acts. Through attachment of place, Forest argued, gay identity could be seen as a kind of ethnicity rather than as a sickness or perversion. In other words place acted to normalize and naturalize the identity of gay people.

Another example of the critical cultural approach to the production of places is Kay Anderson's examination of the construction of Chinatown in Vancouver, Canada (Anderson, K. 1991). Anderson asks how it is that a place known as Chinatown has come to exist in major cities across the world. Many people, she argues, see the existence of Chinatown as evidence of a naturalized connection between Chinese culture and the places that Chinese people settle in around the world. In other words Chinese people arrive and they construct a place full of Chinese restaurants, grocery stores and pagodas. Anderson's argument is that these places cannot simply be read as symbols of essential Chineseness but rather that such places are ideologically constructed as places of difference. In the case of Vancouver she traces the arrival of the Chinese in the west of Canada in response to the discovery of gold and their subsequent work on the railroads, in stores and laundries. Over time they were subjected to a set of discourses among white people about the supposed 'nature' of the Chinese as irredeemably different and inferior. After some time Chinese immigrants began to settle in one area of Vancouver and this clustering alarmed white onlookers. White elites portrayed the Chinese as a form of pollution and disease that threatened white racial purity. By the late 1880s people began to use the word 'Chinatown', a term imported from San Francisco.

> Well before any substantial settlement of Chinese was identified as such in Vancouver, a 'place' for them already had a distinct reality in local vocabulary and culture. 'Had Dante been able to visit Chinatown, San Francisco', said Secretary of State J. Chapleau in 1885, 'he would have added yet darker strokes of horror to his inferno'.   (Anderson 1996, 219)

As Chinese people began to gather around Dupont Street this new 'Chinatown' began to be seen as a natural center of vice and depravity full of dirt, disease and moral failure (opium dens, gambling and prostitution). The racial designation 'Chinese' was seen as synonymous with moral failure and a particular place – Chinatown. For many years the place was put alongside water, sewage and infectious diseases under the responsibility of the municipal sanitary officer.

Anderson shows how 'Chinatown' was not simply a natural reflection of Chinese culture but the result of negotiation with those with the power to define place (the media, government, etc.). More recently this socially constructed place has become a tourist attraction where white tourists can visit the 'exotic other' and enjoy the old ideas and vice and depravity in a sanitized form. Despite the fact that the place is now seen as safe and even as attractive it is still serves to reaffirm a moral order of 'them' and 'us'.

Forest's paper on West Hollywood and Anderson's consideration of Chinatown feature the idea of place at the heart of their analyses. They are not simply papers about particular places – though we do learn about Vancouver and West Hollywood by reading them – but they·are about the way place works in a world of social hierarchies. In the case of West Hollywood, place plays a positive role of affirming gay identity through its inscription in place. Here the linking of place and identity is a political choice of self-affirmation. In the case of Chinatown, place plays a negative role of naturalizing white Western views of Chinese immorality and inferiority by attaching a particular white view of Chinese culture to a place known as Chinatown.

Place for critical cultural geographers from the late 1980s onwards was a concept that needed to be understood through the lens of social and cultural conflict. Issues of race, class, gender, sexuality and a host of other social relations were at the center of this analysis. Place was not simply an outcome of social processes though, it was, once established, a tool in the creation, maintenance and transformation of relations of domination, oppression and exploitation. By fixing Chinese identity in place the cultural and social elites of Vancouver were able to more easily cast Chinese culture and the Chinese themselves in a negative light. By successfully lobbying for the incorporation of West Hollywood, gay people were able to produce an affirmative vision of their own lifestyle.

Place as 'Being-in-the-World' versus Place as Social Construct

Recently Robert Sack, and the philosophers of place Edward Casey and J.E. Malpas, have sought to reinstate a much more fundamental role for place in social life. Their approach can best be explained by contrasting it to the following claim by David Harvey:

> Place, in whatever guise, is like space and time, a social construct. This is the baseline proposition from which I start. The only interesting question that can then be asked is: by what social process(es) is place constructed?
>
> (Harvey 1996, 261)

The assertion of the importance of talking of places as socially constructed nicely outlines the dominant approach to matters of place in contemporary critical human geography. To say a place is socially constructed is to say that it is not natural and given that human forces made a place then human forces can equally importantly undo it. This approach is favored by those with a progressive political agenda as it indicates that if things are one way now, they might be entirely different later. It is the approach taken by the critical human geographers in the previous section. To say something is socially constructed is to say that it is within human power to change it. So what is it that is socially constructed about place? Two things stand out: meaning and materiality.

If we say that New York's Lower East Side is a social construct we are saying that the way we experience that place, the meanings we ascribe to it, come out of a social milieu dominated by Western cultural values and the forces of capitalism. They are also produced by the media, by politicians and by the people who live there. We might have read in the paper about riots in Tompkins Square Park and be (unreasonably) afraid to go there. We might see the graffiti, murals, cafes and shops and think it's an invigorating and diverse place to be. Whatever meaning it appears to have there is little doubt that it comes from 'society'.

To say a place is socially constructed is also to say that the materiality – the very fabric of a place – is a product of society too. The buildings, the parks, the trees that have been planted, the roads and restaurants have literally been built – often for the production of profit but also for a range of other reasons. The community gardens are not 'natural' but have been put there by the tireless efforts of local residents. It is hard to believe that anyone, in a place like the Lower East Side, could think of the place as anything other than a social construct.

In many ways these points seem obvious and we may wonder why Harvey bothers making them at all. But there is another profound way of thinking about place that sees it as something much deeper than a social construct as something irreducible and essential to being human.

Sack, in *Homo Geographicus*, makes the following claim:

> Indeed, privileging the social in modern geography, and especially in the reductionist sense that 'everything is socially constructed,' does as much disservice to geographical analysis as a whole as has privileging the natural in the days of environmental determinism, or concentrating only on the mental or intellectual in some areas of humanistic geography. While one or other may be more important for a particular situation at a particular time, none is determinate of the geographical.   (Sack 1997, 2)

Sack clearly thinks that Harvey is wrong when he asserts that 'the only interesting question that can then be asked: is by what social process(es) is place constructed?' To Sack, place's role in the human world runs a lot deeper than that – it is a force that cannot be reduced to the social, the natural or the cultural. It is, rather, a phenomenon that brings these worlds together and, indeed, in part produced them.

Sack is not the only one to make this point. Consider the words of philosopher J.E. Malpas:

> The idea of place encompasses both the idea of the social activities and institutions that are expressed in and through the structure of a particular place (and which can be seen as partially determinative of that place) and the idea of the physical objects and events in the world (along with the associated causal processes) that constrain, and are sometimes constrained by, those social activities and institutions. There is no doubt that the ordering of a particular place – and the specific way in which a society orders space and time – is not independent of social ordering (inasmuch as it encompasses the social, so place is partially elaborated by means of the social, just as place is also elaborated in relation to orderings deriving from individual subjects and from underlying physical structures). However this does not legitimate the claim that place, space or time are *merely* social constructions. Indeed the social does not exist prior to place nor is it given expression except in and through place – and through spatialised, temporalised ordering ... It is within the structure of place that the very possibility of the social arises.   (Malpas 1999, 35–36)

Note that Malpas, and Sack for that matter, do not deny that specific places are the products of society and culture. They insist, however, that place, in a general sense, adds up to a lot more than that. They point out that society itself is inconceivable without place – that the social (and the cultural) is geographically constructed. On the face of it this does not seem a lot different from the claim that the social and the spatial are 'mutually constitutive' – a claim which is central to some forms of social constructionism. But the claims of Sack and Malpas are different from that because of their claim that the realm of the 'social' has no particular privilege in discussions of place. Malpas looks once more to Heideggar's philosophy of place in which human beings are characterized in terms of their 'being in the world'. This relation between humans and place, Malpas argues is not like apples being in a box but a sense of necessary relation – it is how we are.

> Place is instead that within and with respect to which subjectivity is itself established – place is not founded *on* subjectivity, but is rather that *on which* subjectivity is founded. Thus one does not first have a subject that

apprehends certain features of the world in terms of the idea of place; instead, the structure of subjectivity is given in and through the structure of place.   (Malpas 1999, 35)

This is quite different from the claims of the social constructionists that humans construct both the meaning of place and the material structure of places. Malpas and Sack are arguing that humans cannot construct anything without being first in place – that *place is primary to the construction of meaning and society*. Place is primary because it is the experiential fact of our existence.

The problem for students of place with this view of the world is that it is rather short on empirical detail. If you read the work of Sack, Malpas and Casey you will find few extended accounts of particular places. Because they are talking about place in general it is hard to use specific examples to make the case. Indeed, like Heidegger and his Black Forest Cabin, they tend to use imagined and idealized examples or 'thought experiments'. So what might such a view tell us if we returned to New York's Lower East Side?

First of all it clearly would not tell us much about the processes that went into making the place what it is. It would have more or less nothing to say about the processes of gentrification or the construction of parks in urban areas or the presence of Puerto Rican restaurants. It would not be able to explain the social unrest that has periodically rocked the area. These are all the kinds of things that a Marxist geographer like David Harvey seeks to explain by his insistence that places are socially constructed. But are these, as he claims, the only interesting questions? The place-centered approach of Sack, Malpas and others would suggest that what is going on in the Lower East Side, or anywhere else for that matter, is simply an example of what is going on in all human life – a struggle over the very basis of human experience – the need for place as a bedrock of human meaning and social relations.

These complicated arguments are important and necessary for a thorough understanding of the idea of place in human geography. Perhaps it helps to reconsider the notion of social-construction. All kinds of things are socially constructed – ideas about space and time, particle physics, brain surgery, toothpaste, nuclear bombs, television and fashion are all, with different degrees of obviousness, constructed within particular societies with particular, usually hierarchical, social relations. Some things clearly (at least to this author) are equally clearly not social constructions – gravity, the planet Earth, life and death, glacial moraines. All of these things have socially constructed meanings without which it is impossible to talk about them but the things themselves are there whether we construct them or not. So what kind of thing is place? Place, some would argue, is neither like toothpaste (which once did not exist and in the future will be redundant), nor gravity (which exists completely free of human will or consciousness). It is a construction of humanity but a necessary one – one that human life is impossible to conceive of without. In other words there was no 'place' before there was humanity but once we came into existence then place did too. A future without place is simply inconceivable (unlike a future without toothpaste). Although the social construction of place is not the main theme of Sack and Malpas their arguments suggest that place is a kind of 'necessary social construction' – something we have to construct in order to be human. This is not to say that we have to construct the Lower East Side, Kosovo or the Millennium Dome in all their particularity but that in their absence place would still exist – just different ones.

Place, Practice and Process

Tuan and Relph were not the only geographers who looked to phenomenology in order to develop notions of place. Other 'humanistic' geographers, such as David Seamon were keen to arrive, through phenomenological enquiry, at the essence of geographical phenomena. Place was the central concept but, in Seamon's case, bodily mobility rather then rootedness and authenticity, was the key component to the understanding of place. Following the French phenomenologist Maurice Merleau-Ponty, Seamon fixed on the 'everyday movement in space' – '*any spatial displacement of the body or bodily part initiated by the person himself*. Walking to the mailbox, driving home, going from house to garage, reaching for scissors in a drawer – all these behaviours are examples of movement' (Seamon 1980, 148). As a phenomenological geographer, Seamon was keen to discover the essential experiential character of place through movement. He wanted to transcend specific examples and provide a general account of place as it is embodied.

> Phenomenology ... asks if from the variety of ways which men and women behave in and experience their everyday world there are particular patterns which transcend specific empirical contexts and point to the essential human condition – the irreducible crux of people's life-situations which remains when all non-essentials – cultural context, historical era, personal idiosyncracies – are stripped bare through phenomenological procedures.
> (Seamon 1980, 149)

Seamon believed that most everyday movement takes the form of habit. People drive the same route to work and back everyday without thinking about it. People who have moved house find themselves going to their old house and only realise it when they arrive at the door. People reach for scissors in the drawer while engaging in conversation. Such movements appear to be below the level of conscious scrutiny. The body-subject knows what it is doing – there is an:

> inherent capacity of the body to direct behaviors of the person intelligently, and thus function as a special kind of subject which expresses itself in a preconscious way usually described by such words as 'automatic,' 'habitual,' 'involuntary,' and 'mechanical.'   (Seamon 1980, 155)

Seamon invokes the metaphor of dance in order to describe the sequence of preconscious actions used to complete a particular task such as washing the dishes. He calls such a sequence a body-ballet. When such movements are sustained though a considerable length of time he calls it a 'time-space routine.' This describes the habits of a person as they follow a routine path through the day – driving to work, leaving the kids at school, going to lunch, etc. Seamon also looks beyond the individual body movement to group behavior. When many time-space routines are combined within a particular location a 'place-ballet' emerges which generates, in Seamon's view, a strong sense of place. The mobilities of bodies combine in space and time to produce an existential insideness – a feeling of belonging within the rhythm of life in place.

A 'place-ballet' is an evocative metaphor for our experience of place. It suggests that places are performed on a daily basis through people living their everyday life. Seamon, clearly shares with Relph the notion of being an 'insider' or 'outsider' in a place but the way someone becomes an insider is more specific. It is through participating in these daily performances that we get to know a place and feel part of it. It also suggests that those who do know the routine will appear clumsy and 'out-of-place' simply through the non-conformity of their bodily practice.

One thing that appears to be missing from Seamon's work is any sense of the constraints on people's performances that we would all recognize in places. The fine balancing of constraint and freedom became the subject of geographers influenced by structuration theory – particularly the work of Anthony Giddens and Pierre Bourdieu. In his paper 'Place as Historically Contingent Process' (Pred 1984) Allan Pred announces his dissatisfaction with the prevailing notions of place at the time. He argues that place is too often thought of (by some) in terms of fixed visible and measurable attributes (this many houses, that population, these amenities). As such they become 'little more than frozen scenes for human activity' (Pred 1984, 279). Humanistic geographers do not escape his critical comments as they too 'conceive of place as an inert, experienced scene' (Pred 1984, 279). Pred argues instead for a notion of place that emphasizes change and process. Places are never 'finished' but always 'becoming.' Place is 'what takes place ceaselessly, what contributes to history in a specific context through the creation and utilization of a physical setting' (Pred 1984, 279). This approach is informed by structuration theory – a set of ideas primarily associated with the British sociologist Anthony Giddens. Structuration theory attempts to describe and understand the relations between the overarching structures that influence our lives (ranging from big structures such as capitalism and patriarchy to smaller scales structures such as national and local institutions) and our own ability to exercise agency in our everyday lives. Structurationists say that our actions are neither determined by structures above and beyond us, nor are our actions completely the product of free will. Structures depend on our actions to exist and our actions are given meaning by the structures that lie beyond them. Think of language for example. A language such as English clearly provides a structure of vocabulary and grammar. Stray too far from these rules and we cease to make sense. Having said that no use of language is entirely the product of rules. People use language in different ways. Sometimes these uses do not comply with rules. If this happens enough the structure of language itself begins to change. Without the structure, the individual use of language would have no meaning – in this sense structure enables. Without people practicing the language the structure would be no structure at all – it would be a dead language.

Now think of this in terms of place. We clearly inhabit material landscapes that (excepting rare instances) we had little say in constructing. These landscapes have walls, doors, windows, spaces of flow (roads, paths, bridges, etc.) that we have to negotiate in order to live. We cannot walk through walls and we are unlikely to wander down the middle of the road without endangering our lives. Places also have less concrete structures. Laws and rules pervade place. We cannot park on a double yellow line without risking a fine. We cannot enter private property at will. We are supposed to be at work by nine o'clock. And there are also sets of cultural and social expectations that pervade places. We should not talk loudly to ourselves in public. Women are discouraged from walking alone down dark alleys at night. Young men are not supposed to gather at street corners. All of these structures very from place to place and when we travel we are expected to familiarize ourselves with them.

At a given moment in time, place provides a geographically specific set of structures. But even with layer upon layer of structuring conditions no-one can safely predict what you or I are going to do. We might skip work (or a lecture) and call in sick. The places we have to negotiate are the result of the practices of those who were here before us but this place in the future will be different. It is not a once and for all achieved state. Think of a new green rectangle of lawn in a town of city somewhere. Trees are planted in the middle and two footpaths meet in the exact center to divide the lawn into four smaller rectangles. The lawn is surrounded by roads and buildings. To get across the lawn to the opposite corner the pedestrian is supposed to either walk around the rectangle or use the paths through it. Invariably some people will simply walk across the lawn diagonally. After a few weeks a path will appear – a mud path which becomes the material manifestation of people's desire to take short cuts. Imagine the planners and architects have also provided benches around the circumference as well as steps and a piece of public art in the middle. Soon homeless people use the benches for a night's sleep and skateboarders use the art as an obstacle course. The point is that human agency is not so easily structured and structures themselves are made though the repetition of practices by agents.

Take the place of the university as another example. Universities clearly have a number of more of less established meanings as centers of learning, culture, objectivity, humanistic endeavor and reflection. These have been produced through a long history of learning and institution building going back to the Middle Ages. Over time these places developed separate faculties of arts, sciences, law, medicine, business and others. A way of establishing the authority of 'professors' was devised and built into the structure of lecture halls (with seated students facing a standing professor on a heightened platform). The university you have inherited is, in other words, the product of hundreds of years of the practice of education in particular ways.

> Most modern institutions of education, despite the apparent neutrality of the materials from which they are constructed (red brick, white tile, etc.) carry within themselves implicit ideological assumptions which are literally structured into the architecture itself. The categorisation of knowledge into arts and sciences is reproduced in the faculty system which houses different disciplines in different buildings ... moreover, the hierarchical relationship between teacher and taught is inscribed in the very layout of the lecture theatre with the seating arrangements ... dictate the flow of information and serve to naturalise professorial authority. Thus a whole range of

decisions about what is and is not possible within education have been made, however unconsciously, before the content of individual courses is even decided.   (Hebdige 1988, 12–13)

But it would be wrong to think of the university as a finished place. The traditional arrangement of furniture in the lecture theatre for instance is frequently ignored in small classes where dissatisfied students or a professor rearrange chairs into circles or other more inclusive spatial arrangements. Over time this might mean that more and more university rooms are built with increasing amounts of moveable furniture. Perhaps even more revolutionary are the opportunities provided by the Internet and 'distance learning' that makes formal 'placed' education increasingly redundant. The university as a place, then, is not complete. In general places are never complete, finished or bounded but are always becoming – in process.

It is this sense of process and the relations of structure and agency in place that is the subject of Pred's (1984) paper. Places are never finished but always the result of processes and practices. As such places need to be studied in terms of the 'dominant institutional projects', the individual biographies of people negotiating a place and the way in which a sense of place is developed though the interaction of structure and agency. In terms of our imaginary park suitable empirical studies might include an examination of the intentions and practices of those who made the park in the first place, the way in which skateboarders, the homeless or the local office workers who eat lunch there use the place and the way in which the meanings of the park change and are negotiated over time.

The work of Nigel Thrift has continued to develop notions of process and practice in human geography. Along with Allan Pred and Derek Gregory he was instrumental in introducing structuration theory to geography (Thrift 1983; Gregory 1998). More recently Thrift has developed what he calls 'non-representational theory' (Thrift 1997; Thrift 1996) – an approach which emphasizes events and practices rather than the more orthodox focus (within cultural geography) on interpretation and representation. Like David Seamon before him Thrift leans on the work of Maurice Merleau-Ponty in suggesting that the body has for too long been subordinated to the head in social and cultural geography (as well as the wider social sciences). If we focus on the way we do things, Thrift argues, we get at a primal relationship with the world that is more embodied and less abstract. Place, then, needs to be understood as an embodied relationship with the world. Places are constructed by people doing things and in this sense are never 'finished' but are constantly being performed.

A related way of looking a place and practice is given by Edward Soja. Soja has developed his notion of the 'trialectics of spatiality' by developing the work of the French theorist Henri Lefebvre (Soja 1989, Soja 1999, Lefebvre 1991). His starting point is a critique of the binary notions of spatiality which have been at the center of geographical discourse. These include the oppositions of objectivity versus subjectivity, material versus mental, real versus imagined and space versus place. To challenge all of these binaries he writes of 'thirdspace.' Thirdspace is lived space and it interrupts a distinction between perceived space and spatial practices. Firstspace is the term he uses to describe empirically measurable and mappable phenomena. This is the traditional domain of human geography – the spatial outcome of social processes. Secondspace is conceived space – space which is subjective and imagined – the domain of representations and image. This corresponds of many people's notion of place – a felt and cared for center of meaning. Secondspace therefore, corresponds to the humanist critique of positivist conception of space. Soja and Lefebvre's critique is that these two ways of thinking, that correspond to the binaries of objective/subjective; material/mental; real/imagined and so on have tended to be seen as the whole story. Thirdspace, or lived space is therefore a different way of thinking. Thirdspace is practiced and lived rather than simply being material (conceived) or mental (perceived). This focus on the lived world does seem to provide theoretical groundwork for thinking about a politics of place based on place as lived, practiced and inhabited space.

In these terms places are never established. They only operate through constant and reiterative practice. Universities, to return to our example, are both produced and producing. Universities would be nothing if they were not inhabited by people conforming to expectations about what people do at university – visiting the library, taking exams, attending class. Indeed they are performed. Every single day, everywhere, universities, like all places, need to be reproduced. On the other hand we do not perform our practices in vacuums. We are surrounded by the material form of places and their contingent meanings. There is nothing natural or immutable about them – they are social products but they do provide the context for out practice. It would be crazy for us to walk down the middle of a busy street or talk loudly to ourselves in the library.

One of the books that has proved most useful in thinking about the issue of practice in relation to space and place is Michel de Certeau's account of *The Practice of Everyday Life* (de Certeau 1984). Confusingly for geographers de Certeau uses space and place in a way that stands the normal distinction on its head. To de Certeau place is the empty grid over which practice occurs while space is what is created by practice. The central tension in de Certeau's work is between a systemic grammar of space – an order that we inhabit and is not constructed by us – on the one hand and our ability to use this grammar in ways which are not predetermined. The guiding metaphor here is language. While we have to use the rules and structures of language to make sense – the ways we do this in practice are almost infinite. The same applies to place. While we live in places that come pre-structured – embedded with particular interests in the context of unequal power relations – those places are not operational without practice in them. Think of a pedestrian. Pedestrians do not walk though walls but they do behave in unquantifiable ways. In de Certeau's terms they fill the streets with the 'forests of their desires and goals' (de Certeau 1984, xxi). Practice is thus a tactical art that plays with the structures of place that are provided. The mobile world of practice teases apart place in its orthodox form.

The work of Seamon, Pred, Thrift, de Certeau and others show us how place is constituted though reiterative social practice – place is made and remade on a daily basis. Place provides a template for practice – an unstable stage for performance. Thinking of place as performed and practiced can help us think of place in radically open and non-essentialized ways where place is constantly struggled over and reimagined in practical ways. Place is the raw material for the creative production of identity rather than an *a priori* label of identity. Place provides the conditions of possibility for creative social practice. Place in this sense becomes an event rather than a secure ontological thing rooted in notions of the authentic. Place as an event is marked by openness and change rather than bounded-ness and permanence.

Place, Openness and Change

The kind of place at the center of much of humanistic geography is very much a place of rootedness and authenticity. In Harvey's discussion of place this meaning is retained but becomes a symbol of reactionary exclusivity. As long as place signifies a tight and relatively immobile connection between a groups of people and a site then it will be constantly implicated in the construction of 'us' (people who belong in a place) and 'them' (people who do not). In this way outsiders are constructed. In Harvey's work this produces a fairly damning critique of place as it is normally understood (see Chapter 3 for more on this).

But place need not be thought of in such introverted and exclusionary terms. Doreen Massey rejects this notion of place in her
development of the idea of a 'progressive'or 'global' sense of place.
She has encouraged us to think of place in a way that combines
bodies, objects and flows in new ways. As Arturo Escobar has argued
'places gather things, thoughts, and memories in particular configura-
tions' (Escobar 2001, 143). Place in this sense becomes an event rather
than a secure ontological thing rooted in notions of the authentic.
Place as an event is marked by openness and change rather than
boundedness and permanence. This significantly alters the value put
on place as it is constructed from the outside rather from the inside.
We will consider Massey's important definition of a 'global (or progressive) sense of place' in the next chapter in more depth. But she is
not the only one considering how places are constructed by objects
and processes from outside.

The artist and commentator Lucy Lippard has made similar
observations in her book *The Lure of the Local.*

> Inherent in the local is the concept of place – a portion of land/town/
> cityscape seen from the inside, the resonance of a specific location that is
> known and familiar ... Place is latitudinal and longitudinal within the map
> of a person's life. It is temporal and spatial, personal and political. A layered
> location replete with human histories and memories, place has width as
> well as depth. It is about connections, what surrounds it, what formed it,
> what happened there, what will happen there.   (Lippard 1997, 7)

Here Lippard agrees with Massey's contention that places are 'about
connections' but makes more of the layering of histories which
sediment in place and become the bedrock for future action.

Environmental historians have also developed ways of thinking
about place that mesh well with Massey's progressive sense of place.
William Cronon's book *Nature's Metropolis*, for instance, reveals how
Chicago was constructed through its relationship with a rural
hinterland (Cronon 1991). Cronon traces the voyages of corn, timber,
meat and other products from the countryside into the metropolis and
shows how the movements in and out of place produce both new
material landscapes, new sets of social relations and new relations
between people and 'nature.' He performs a similar analysis of a small
ghost town in Alaska in a wonderful essay called 'Kennecott Journey:
The Paths out of Town.'

In his essay Cronon visits Kennecott, a long deserted town north of
Valdez in South Central Alaska. He described the ruins of place in
great detail – particularly its huge, spectacularly rambling crushing
mill that provided so much employment for its earlier residents.

It is a ghost factory in a ghost town, yet its haunting could have almost have begun yesterday. In the bunkhouse where the millmen slept and ate, linen is still on the beds, and plates are still on the cafeteria tables. Open account books lie scattered around the store-rooms and offices, protected from decay only by the coldness of the northern climate. Even the machinery is remarkably well preserved: Lift the gears of the sifting mechanisms, and beautifully clear oil still bathes the gears with lubricant. (Cronon 1992, 30)

Cronon's essay explores what made this place a booming and vibrant town for a little more than thirty years and what subsequently led to its downfall. In order to do this he traces the links between Kennecott and other places. Between 1911 and 1938 Kennecott thrived because of the copper that had been discovered there – the richest vein the world had ever seen. The 1930s saw the bottom fall out of the copper market and the rich vein of copper was, anyway, beginning to yield less material. In 1938 the Kennecott Copper Company closed all its Alaskan mines and moved operations to other sites in North and South America.

'What' Cronon asks 'is one to make of this place and of the memories that lie so visibly on the landscape?' (Cronon 1992, 32). His answer is to trace the connections between Kennecott and the rest of the world. These connections include 'the ecology of people as organisms sharing the universe with many other organisms, the political economy of people as social beings reshaping nature and one another to produce their collective life, and the cultural values of people as storytelling creatures struggling to find meaning of their place in the world' (Cronon 1992, 32).

As we seek to understand Kennecott, the questions we ask must show us the paths out of town – the connections between this lonely place and the rest of the world – for only by walking those paths can we reconnect his ghost community to the circumstances that created it. (Cronon 1992, 33)

There are many 'paths out of town'. One is that produced by the need to eat food in a place that does not provide much sustenance. As soon as there were significant numbers of non-native people in Kennecott then food had to be imported.

When people exchange things in their immediate vicinity for things that can only be obtained elsewhere, they impose a new set of meanings on the local landscape and connect it to the wider world. These increase the chance that the local environment will begin to change in response to outside forces, so that trade becomes a powerful new source of ecological change. (Cronon 1992, 37)

Kennecott soon became part of ever-wider networks of exchange. Russian traders started to operate along the coast of Alaska and thus integrated even interior Alaska into a large Eurasian market for furs.

> Trade linked the resources of one ecosystem with the human demands of another. Alaskan villages that had not sugar, alcohol, or tobacco obtained such things by trading with communities that had no furs. The net result was to redefine the resources of the Alaskan landscape, pushing them beyond the needs of the local subsistence into the realm of the market, where any good could be transformed into any other. At the same time the act of economic consumption came to be increasingly separated from the place of ecological production, distancing people from the consequences of their own acts and desires.   (Cronon 1992, 38–39)

Cronon traces the development of trade between the native population and the arriving military expeditions. The key resource, of course, was copper. While the native population of Kennecott saw copper as interesting for its color and the fact that they could make it into weapons, tools and jewelry they were not aware of its ability to conduct electricity and had little idea of its value to American industry. The huge mines of Kennecott and the town that surrounded it were focused on this resource. Along with the new population came new foods and plant species such as turnips and cabbages. Local game was soon hunted to exhaustion. Food was a problem. In order to supply the growing population with nutrition a railroad was built. In order for the new population to mine the copper they had to import new definitions of property – thus a legal landscape was imported along with the turnips. The native population had no concept of static property or place. They were nomadic and would move according to the availability of resources. This lifestyle, Cronon writes, 'left them little concerned with drawing sharp property boundaries upon the landscape' the newcomers 'had in mind a completely different way of owning and occupying the terrain. And therein lay the origin of the community called Kennecott' (Cronon 1992, 42). So the irony of Kennecott – a place produced by its connections – was that the idea of place itself was imported from outside. Place based on property and boundaries.

To understand the place called Kennecott – and by extension any place – Cronon argues, we must pay attention to its connections. Kennecott became possible at the moment it appeared because connections made it possible. Everything the residents consumed depended upon a prior history in other places from the development of salmon canneries on the Alaskan shoreline to the coffee and sugar trade with the tropics. 'At no prior moment in the history of the West would it have been possible for capitalists in New York to hire engineers and workers in Alaska to construct a railroad, mine, and crushing mill deep in the interior of that remote territory so that the nation's cities could purchase a metal they hardly knew they needed just a half century before' (Cronon 1992, 49). Similarly the demise of Kennecott owes everything to the emergence of cheaper copper industries in South America and the dictates and foibles of a truly global economy.

Cronon's work is not written as theory. Like many environmental historians he uses narrative to make us think about the issues at hand. But what his journey to Kennecott tells us is that places need to be understood as sites that are connected to others around the world in constantly evolving networks which are social, cultural and natural/ environmental. Places need to be understood through the paths that lead in and out. Similar stories could be written about many, if not all, places around the world and geographers have begun to think in very similar terms. Matthew Gandy has explored how New York City has been constructed through its relationship to nature (Gandy 2002) and Dan Clayton has explored the construction of British Columbia through the passages of a whole array of imperial and local travelers to and through the place (Clayton 2000).

The End of Place?

The very processes Cronon writes about – the way in which places are tied into global flows of people, meanings and things – has led some to perceive an accelerating erosion of place. A combination of mass communication, increased mobility and a consumer society has been blamed for a rapidly accelerating homogenization of the world. More and more of our lives, it has been argued, take place in spaces that could be anywhere – that look, feel, sound and smell the same wherever in the globe we may be. Fast food outlets, shopping malls, airports, high street shops and hotels are all more or less the same wherever we go. These are spaces that seem detached from the local environment and tell us nothing about the particular locality in which they are located. The meaning that provides the sense of attachment to place has been radically thinned out.

This issue of the erosion of place was a central theme of humanistic geographer Edward Relph's book *Place and Placelessness*. Relph, you will recall, was one of the geographers who brought the issue of place to the attention of geographers in a sustained way. Bear in mind that he was writing long before the level of geographical homogenization we (in the West) now experience was quite so ubiquitous. Relph was concerned that it was becoming increasingly difficult for people to feel connected to the world through place. Relph makes the distinction between the experience of insideness and outsideness in the human experience of place. 'To be inside a place is to belong to it and identify with it, and the more profoundly inside you are the stronger is the identity with the place' (Relph 1976, 49). At the opposite extreme, existential outsideness involves the alienation from place which is the antithesis of an unreflective sense of belonging that comes from being an existential insider.

A key term for Relph (developing Heidegger's notion of 'dwelling') is 'authenticity'. Authenticity means a genuine and sincere attitude, 'As a form of existence authenticity consists of a complete awareness and acceptance of responsibility for your own existence' (Relph 1976, 78). An existential insider has an authentic attitude to a place which is likely to be authentic. An inauthentic attitude to place, on the other hand:

> is essentially no sense of place, for it involves no awareness of the deep and symbolic significances of places and no appreciation of their identities. It is merely an attitude which is socially convenient and acceptable – an uncritically accepted stereotype, an intellectual of aesthetic fashion that can be adopted without real involvement.   (Relph 1976, 82)

In the modern world, Relph argues that we are surrounded by a general condition of creeping placelessness marked by an inability to have authentic relationships to place because the new placelessness does not allow people to become existential insiders.

> An inauthentic attitude towards places is transmitted through a number of processes, or perhaps more accurately 'media', which directly or indirectly encourage 'placelessness', that is, a weakening of the identity of places to the point where they not only look alike and feel alike and offer the same bland possibilities for experience.   (Relph 1976, 90)

The processes that lead to this are various and include the ubiquity of mass communication and culture as well as big business and central authority. Tourism, Relph writes, is particularly to blame as it encourages the disneyfication, museumization, and futurization of places.

One of the main culprits here is mobility. Relph makes a direct connection between inauthentic placelessness and mobility by claiming that the mobility of American homeowners (changing home every three years) reduces the significance of home and thus plays a major role in the growing problem of placelessness in the (American) modern world. Another factor in the creation of placelessness is, in Relph's view, modern travel/tourism which encourages a fascination with the 'machinery and paraphernalia of travel ... itself. In short, where someone goes is less important than the act and style of going' (Relph 1976). A place like Disneyworld represents the epitome of placelessness constructed, as it is, purely for outsiders and now reproduced across the globe in France and Japan.

Superhighways also play their part in the destruction of place as they do not connect places and are separated from the surrounding landscape – they 'start everywhere and lead nowhere' (Relph 1976). Before the highways the railways were the culprits destroying authentic senses of place:

> Roads, railways, airports, cutting across or imposed on the landscape rather than developing with it, are not only features of placelessness in their own right, but, by making possible the mass movement of people with all their fashions and habits, have encouraged the spread of placelessness well beyond their immediate impacts. (Relph 1976, 90)

Relph connects various forms of increased mobility to what he calls 'mass culture' and mass values which again dilute authentic relations to place. Places become 'other directed' and more alike across a globe of transient connections. Mobility and mass culture lead to irrational and shallow landscapes.

In a similar way the anthropologist Marc Augé has argued that the facts of postmodernity (he refers to supermodernity) point to a need for a radical rethinking of the notion of place (Augé 1995). Place, he argues, has traditionally been thought of as a fantasy of a 'society anchored since time immemorial in the permanence of an intact soil.' Augé's argument is that such places are receding in importance and being replaced by 'non-places.'

> The multiplication of what we may call empirical non-places is characteristic of the contemporary world. Spaces of circulation (freeways, airways), consumption (department stores, supermarkets), and communication (telephones, faxes, television, cable networks) are taking up more room all over the earth today. They are spaces where people coexist or cohabit without living together. (Augé 1999: 110).

Non-places are sites marked by their transience – the preponderance of mobility. Auge's use of the name non-place does not have the same

Figure 2.1 *Disneyworld, Orlando, Florida. Authors have argued that tourist places such as Disneyworld are not real places but 'placeless' places or 'pseudo-places' with no real history and no sense of belonging. (Photo by author)*

negative moral connotations as Relph's 'placelessness.' By non-place Augé is referring to sites marked by the 'fleeting, the temporary and ephemeral.' Non-places include freeways, airports, supermarkets – sites where particular histories and traditions are not (allegedly) relevant – unrooted places marked by mobility and travel. Non-place is essentially the space of travelers. Augé's arguments force theorists of culture to reconsider the theory and method of their disciplines. While conventionally figured places demand thoughts which reflect assumed boundaries and traditions, non-places demand new mobile ways of thinking.

Tuan too reflected on the effects of a mobile world on the experience of place in modernity. He picks out the figure of the business man as a symbol of this new world:

> He moves around so much that places for him tend to lose their special character. What are his significant places? The home is in the suburb. He lives there, but home is not wholly divorced from work. It is occasionally a showplace for the lavish entertainment of colleagues and business associates. . . . The executive takes periodic trips abroad, combining business with pleasure. He stays at the same hotel, or with the same friends, in Milan, and again in Barbados. The circuits of movement are complex.
>
> (Tuan 1977, 183)

Figure 2.2 *A village in Dartmoor, England. When people think and write about place they often fix on old small places that seem 'authentic' such as this village in Dartmoor. Think, for instance, of the way Heidegger wrote about a cabin in the Black Forest to make his argument about 'being-in-the-world'. (Photo by author)*

Figure 2.3 *Baltimore-Washington International Airport. Airports, by contrast are frequently described as non-places or placeless. They do not appear to have histories and are marked by transience and mobility. (Photo by author)*

This kind of life, Tuan goes on, leads inevitably to a superficial sense of place:

> Abstract knowledge *about* a place can be acquired in short order if one is diligent. The visual quality of an environment is quickly tallied if one has the artist's eye. But the 'feel' of a place takes longer to acquire. It is made up of experiences, mostly fleeting and undramatic, repeated day after day and over the span of years.   (Tuan 1977, 183)

Nigel Thrift describes mobility as a structure of feeling that emerged with modernity and has attained new characteristics as we approached the twenty-first century. The focus of his argument is on developing technologies and 'machine complexes' starting with the stage coach and ending (provisionally) with the Internet. By 1994, when he wrote the essay, developments in speed, light and power had reached such a point that they had combined and fused with people and changed everything. Towards the end of his essay he lays out some of the consequences of this structure of feeling for human geography. One of these concerns place.

> What is place in this 'in-between' world? The short answer is – compromised: permanently in a state of enunciation, between addresses, always deferred. Place are 'stages of intensity'. Traces of movement, speed and circulation. One might read this depiction of 'almost places' ... in Baudrillardean terms as a world of third-order simulacra, where encroaching pseudo-places have finally advanced to eliminate places altogether. Or one might record places ... as strategic installations, fixed addresses that capture traffic. Or, finally, one might read them ... as frames for varying practices of space, time and speed.   (Thrift 1994, 212–13)

Gone are the implicit moral judgements of inauthenticity and lack of commitment. At worst this reading of mobility and place is neutral and at best it is a positive celebration of mobile worlds. Thrift sees mobility as a mark of all of life in an increasingly speeded up world. The study of the modern world is a study of velocities and vectors. Rather than comparing mobility to place, mobilities are placed in relation to each other. Place in this world seems increasingly redundant.

Or perhaps not. Just as place (at least in the form of relatively stable wholes firmly rooted in the past) appears to be more or less irrelevant it seems to be the word on many people's lips. Advertisers sell us places or ways to make places. Travel brochures encourage us to get to know places. Politicians and artists lament the loss of place and strive to produce new ones. Urban dwellers leave the city to look for a place in the country where life will slow down and they can raise some chickens. Perhaps, In Joni Mitchell's words 'we don't know what we've got 'till it's gone, they paved paradise and put up a parking lot'.

Clearly if place is the very bedrock of our humanity, as some have claimed, then it cannot have vanished because it is a necessary part of the human condition. Places have certainly changed though and this has produced anxiety. Lucy Lippard, a thoughtful writer on place, has reflected on what place might mean in the speeded up world we inhabit. Here the effect of mobility on place is less extreme than the likes of Relph, Augé and Thrift, from their varying perspectives would have us believe.

> Most of us move around a lot, but when we move we often come into contact with those who haven't moved around, or have come from different places. This should give us a better understanding of difference (though it will always be impossible to understand everything about difference). Each time we enter a new place, we become one of the ingredients of an existing hybridity, which is really what all 'local places' consist of. (Lippard 1997, 5–6)

Here Lippard suggests that mobility and place go hand in hand as places are always already hybrid anyway. By moving through, between and around them we are simply adding to the mix. She suggests that the 'pull of place' continues to operate in all of us as the 'geographical component of the psychological need to belong some-where, one antidote to a prevailing alienation' (Lippard 1997, 7). Even in the age of a 'restless, multitraditional people' she argues, and 'even as the power of place is diminished and often lost, it continues – as an absence – to define culture and identity. It also continues – as a presence – to change the way we live' (Lippard 1997, 20).

Conclusions: Versions of Place

In this chapter we have explored the changing role of place in human geography and beyond. We have seen how place, in a common-sense way, has always been central to the discipline but relatively un-developed as an idea until the 1970s and the emergence of humanistic geography founded on phenomenology. Writers such as Tuan and Relph, and later Sack and Malpas, developed the idea of place as a central meaningful component in human life – a center of meaning and field of care that formed the basis for human interaction. Critical human geographers, informed by Marxism, feminism and cultural studies

were keen to show how places were socially constructed in contexts of unequal power relations and how they represented relations of domination and exploitation. Throughout these debates geographers such as Seamon, Pred, Thrift and Massey have insisted that places should not be thought of in terms of stasis and boundedness but are instead the product of processes that extend well beyond the confines of a particular place. Sometimes, though, these processes, particularly the mobility of people objects and ideas, appear to undermine place and produce a kind of placelessness or non-place. Yet still place seems to be an important factor in our experience of the world.

Place is clearly a complicated concept. It is all the more confusing because, at first glance, it appears to be obvious and common-sense. It is worth thinking back over the various approaches to place in this chapter to consider the different ways different geographers have written about place. In many ways they appear to be writing about quite different things. Regional geographers talk about places as discrete areas of land with their own ways of life. Humanists write of place as a fundamental way of being in the world. Radical geographers investigate the way places are constructed as reflections of power. Those involved in variations of structuration theory see places as parts of the process of the reproduction of society. Is it possible that they all hold nuggets of value for contemporary human geography? Or do they cancel each other out? Is there one 'place' at the center of the debate?

The central argument about place in geography and beyond seems to be between those who write of place in terms of individual places – their locations, their boundaries and their associated meanings and practices (regional geographers, specific accounts of the politics of particular places, etc.) – and those who want to argue for a deeper primal sense of place (humanistic geographers, philosophers of place). Maybe both exist. The kinds of places we inhabit – favorite rooms, neighborhoods, nations – are all indeed analysable as social products – as political outcomes and tools in the ongoing struggles between sectors of society. And, indeed, they are all describable in the way regional geographers have described them in the past. But perhaps these places are all instances or examples of a deeper sense that humanity has to exist in place. It would be wrong to romanticize this sense of place as always rosy and 'homelike' (in the idealized sense of home). Some places are evil, oppressive and exploitative. But they are still the way we experience the world – through and in place. And perhaps it is because place is so primal to human existence that it becomes such a powerful political force in its socially constructed forms. It is impossible, after all, to think of a world without place.

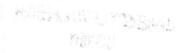

Through the history of the idea of place it is possible to see (at least) three levels at which place is approached.

1. A descriptive approach to place. This approach most closely resembles the common-sense idea of the world being a set of places each of which can be studied as a unique and particular entity. This *ideographic* approach to place was the one taken by regional geographers but continues to the present day. The concern here is with the distinctiveness and particularity of places. A geographer taking this approach might want to research and write about 'The Geography of the North of England' or 'The Soul of San Francisco'.

2. A social constructionist approach to place. This approach is still interested in the particularity of places but only as instances of more general underlying social processes. Marxists, feminists and post-structuralists might take this approach to place. Looking at the social construction of place involves explaining the unique attributes of a place (say the Docklands of London or the Baltimore harbor) by showing how these places are instances of wider processes of the construction of place in general under conditions of capitalism, patriarchy, heterosexism, post-colonialism and a host of other structural conditions (Anderson, K. 1991; Clayton 2000; Forest 1995; Till 1993).

3. A phenomenological approach of place. This approach is not particularly interested in the unique attributes of particular places nor is it primarily concerned with the kinds of social forces that are involved in the construction of particular places. Rather it seeks to define the essence of human existence as one that is necessarily and importantly 'in-place'. This approach is less concerned with 'places' and more interested in 'Place'. Humanistic geographers, neo-humanists and phenomenological philosophers all take this approach to place (Sack 1997; Malpas 1999; Casey 1998; Tuan 1974a).

These three levels should not be seen as discrete sets as there is clearly some overlap between them. Broadly speaking they represent three levels of 'depth' in approaches to place with the level one representing a concern with the surface of the world as we see it and level three representing a deep universal sense of what place means to humanity. It would be wrong however to think that these correspond in some easy way to 'importance'. Research at all three levels (and the ones in between) are important and necessary to understand the full complexity of the role of place in human life.

3

Reading 'A Global Sense of Place'

The purpose of this chapter is to consider, in some depth, how place has been thought through in a key reading from the discipline. Of course there are many possible readings and many of them have been mentioned in previous chapters. Doreen Massey's paper 'A Global Sense of Place' has been widely cited as a plea for a new conceptualization of place as open and hybrid – a product of interconnecting flows – of routes rather then roots. This extroverted notion of place calls into question the whole history of place as a center of meaning connected to a rooted and 'authentic' sense of identity forever challenged by mobility. It also makes a critical intervention into the widely held notions of the erosion of place through globalization and time-space compression. I have chosen this paper, then, because it allows for reflection on all of the central themes that surround the notion of place and points towards a new way of thinking. Looking at this paper alone, however, would not do justice to the complexity and political urgency of the debates around place. It needs to be understood in its intellectual and historical context. For this reason the chapter also includes excerpts from David Harvey's chapter 'From Space to Place and Back Again' from his book *Justice, Nature and the Geography of Difference* (1996). Finally a nuanced response to both of these papers is given by Jon May in his paper 'Globalization and the Politics of Place' (1996).

Historical Context

'A Global Sense of Place' was published in 1991 and republished in 1994 in Massey's book *Space, Place and Gender*. It has also been anthologized in the 1997 collection *Reading Human Geography* (Barnes and Gregory 1997) and, in a slightly different form, in the 1993 collection *Mapping the Futures* (Bird *et al.* 1993). This was a time, as Massey writes herself, when the world was experiencing rapid 'globalization'. Transport, communications and institutional support for global capital (the World Bank, the International Monetary Fund, etc.) had conspired to seemingly make places less important – less unique. Anti-globalization protests were small and unreported until the latter part of the 1990s. In the UK, more and more people flew abroad for holidays while the high street at home seemed increasingly homogenous as global chains such as MacDonalds appeared across the globe. Alongside this apparent homogenization a new kind of diversity was formed in the western world. Clothes came from around the world (labels read 'product of more than one country'), 'ethnic' restaurants expanded from the expected Chinese and Indian (in the UK) examples to include Mexican, Vietnamese or Mongolian (for instance). Supermarkets displayed a bewildering array of foodstuffs that often needed elaborate explanations on a nearby sign ('how to use a star fruit'). It suddenly became possible to buy fifteen varieties of rice from around the world. It seemed that two complimentary changes were occurring at a global scale – the repetition of outlets owned by multinational corporations everywhere across the globe (homogenization) and the flowering of a diverse array of international cultural products in urban areas everywhere. Both of these appeared to threaten the notion of unique places.

The early 1990s also witnessed a number of violent place-based uprisings usually based on the desires of oppressed minorities for nationhood or some other form of regional autonomy. The one that was most often portrayed in the Western media was the break up of Yugoslavia and the horrors of ethnic cleansing that accompanied it. The period also saw the rise of Islamic fundamentalism – such as the success of the Taliban in Afghanistan – which was, in part, a reaction to globalization and the perceived cultural imperialism of the United States and Europe. On a smaller scale the United States, in particular, was witnessing a rapid proliferation of 'gated communities' – specially managed places to live with extremely tight security designed to protect against the imagined horrors of city life (Till 1993). The heritage industry was also active, attempting to package places and their histories in a sanitized way in order to attract tourists and their money. So at many scales place was very much on the agenda either through its apparent homogenization or through various attempts to create places from the nation to the heritage park.

It was in this context that Doreen Massey and David Harvey engaged in quite different analyses of the idea of place in the contemporary world and what it might mean. As we will see, Harvey, whose paper 'From Space to Place and Back Again' was first given at a conference at the Tate Gallery in 1990, was quite disturbed by the emergence of a politics of place that could often be quite reactionary and exclusionary – using place to define one group of people over and against others. Massey, on the other hand, sought to redefine place as a much more open and progressive force in the world. We will start with Harvey.

Harvey on Place

David Harvey, in his paper 'From Space to Place and Back Again' begins with an example from his home town of Baltimore to make his more abstract arguments about place.

> On Sunday August 14, 1994 a brutal double murder occurred in Guilford. An elderly white couple, both distinguished physicians but now retired in their 80s, were found in their bed bludgeoned to death with a baseball bat. Murder is no stranger to Baltimore (the rate for the city is one a day). But in the eyes of the media the Guilford killings were special. The main local newspaper – the *Baltimore Sun* – devoted full-page coverage to them when most other murders received nominal attention. The media dwelt at length on how this was the third such incident in Guilford in recent months and that something plainly had to be done to protect the community if it was to survive. The solution that had long been pressed by the Guilford Community Association was to turn Guilford into a gated community with restricted access.   (Harvey 1996, 292)

Harvey reports how the media turned to the views of Oscar Newman, the author of *Defensible Space* (1972) who suggested that the production of gated communities was one way to secure neighborhoods against crimes such as prostitution, drug dealing and mugging. Gated communities are essentially collections of houses (and sometimes shops and leisure services) with a wall around them and one or two ways in and out. These entrances/exits can then be policed by private security forces, cctv and other forms of surveillance. Residents have passes to allow them in and out and guests have to be recorded. In the case of Guilford the production of the gated community would effectively separate a white community (in Guilford) from a black community (beyond).

> The whole tenor of the *Sun's* report implied ... that crime was an African-American and 'underclass' habit and that therefore the construction of barriers against people of color and of low income, however regrettable, might be justifiable as a means to secure a defensible space of 'community' for an affluent white middle-class population that might otherwise flee the city. *Place* had to be secured against the uncontrolled vectors of spatiality.
>
> (Harvey 1996, 292)

As it turned out, the murders in Guilford were not committed by some random intruder from the world beyond but by the grandson of the couple.

Here Harvey pits the idea of place (as a secure bounded community) against what he calls the 'uncontrolled vectors of spatiality'. As is often the case in the history of geography place stands against fluidity and flux which are portrayed as threatening. Note it is not Harvey who is saying that place can be a secure haven in an unpredictable world. He is simply observing that this is how the argument is constructed in the *Baltimore Sun*. Nonetheless his choice of this example does indicate something of the way he uses place in his own work.

> So what kind of *place* is Guilford? It has a name, a boundary, and distinctive social and physical qualities. It has achieved a certain kind of 'permanence' in the midst of the fluxes and flows of urban life. Protection of this permanence has become a political-economic project not only for Guilford residents but also for a wide range of institutions in the city (government, the media, and finance in particular). And it has a discursive/symbolic meaning well beyond that of mere location, so that events that occur there have a particular significance, as signified by the response in the press and the media to the murders. Guilford plainly fits into cartographies of struggle, power, and discourse in Baltimore city in very special ways. But different maps locate it differently, as the two contrasting reports in the *Sun* clearly indicated.
>
> (Harvey 1996, 293)

Here Harvey uses the well rehearsed and familiar characteristics of place ('a discursive/symbolic meaning well beyond that of mere location') to argue that it is just such characteristics that become important in the attempts of privileged groups in Baltimore to further 'fix' Guilford as a secure white bourgeois place. It is important to bear in mind Harvey's choice of example when exploring the rest of his paper on the nature of place. One aspect of place that the example does clearly show (and this was Harvey's intention) is that places don't just exist but that they are always and continually being socially constructed by powerful institutional forces in society.

> Place, in whatever guise, is like space and time, a social construct. This is the baseline proposition from which I start. The only interesting question that can then be asked: is by what social process(es) is place constructed? There are two ways to get a fix on that problem. The first is to recapitulate what the relational view of space-time tells us:
>
>> entities achieve relative stability in both their bounding and their internal ordering of processes creating space, for a time. Such permanences come to occupy a piece of space in an exclusive way (for a time) and thereby define a place – their place – (for a time). The process of place formation is a process of carving out 'permanences' from the flow of processes creating spatio-temporality. But the 'permanences' – no matter how solid they may seem – are not eternal but always subject to time as 'perpetual perishing.' They are contingent on processes of creation, sustenance and dissolution.
>>
>> (Above, 261)
>
> A double meaning can, therefore, be given to place as (a) a mere position of location within a map of space-time constituted within some social process of (b) an entity or 'permanence' occurring within and transformative of the construction of space-time ... The difference in meanings is between putting down a marker such as 30.03ºS and 51.10ºW on a map of the globe or naming the city of Porto Alegre in the state of Rio Grande do Sul in Brazil. (Harvey 1996, 293–294)

So place for Harvey, is a conditional form of 'permanence' in the flow of space and time. Although using a completely different language this recalls Tuan's observation that 'if we think of space as that which allows movement, then place is pause; each pause in movement makes it possible for location to be transformed into place' (Tuan 1977, 6). But Harvey is more interested in the political world than Tuan and the pause that comes with place allows not so much a sense of existential belonging but an opportunity to mark particular boundaries and constitute particular forms of local government and social power. Harvey's attention is focused on the 'political economy of place construction under capitalism'.

Capital is relatively free to move around the globe at the press of a button. Capital is mobile. Place, on the other hand, is fixed. This tension between mobile capital and fixed place is fundamental for

Harvey. The 'permanence' of place is a form of investment in fixity. Infrastructures have to be built that cannot readily be moved at a moment's notice.

> The tension between place-bound fixity and spatial mobility of capital erupts into generalized crisis, however, when the landscape shaped in relation to a certain phase of development (capitalist or pre-capitalist) becomes a barrier to further accumulation. The geographical configuration of places must then be reshaped around new transport and communications systems and physical infrastructures, new centers and styles of production and consumption, new agglomerations of labor power, and modified social infrastructures ... Old places ... have to be devalued, destroyed, and redeveloped while new places are created. The cathedral city becomes a heritage center, the mining community becomes a ghost town, the old industrial center is deindustrialised, speculative boom towns or gentrified neighbourhoods arise on the frontier of capitalist development or out of the ashes of deindustrialised communities   (Harvey 1996, 296)

So the permanence of place and the mobility of capital are always in tension and places are constantly having to adapt to conditions beyond their boundaries. Places compete to get a share of the mobile capital – encouraging companies to invest in their particular form of fixity. Places have to sell themselves as good places to live and work and invest (Kearns and Philo 1993).

It is this mobility of capital that many see as the prime force of globalization and the main reason for the perceived homogenization of places around the world. As capital becomes more mobile and mass communication more ubiquitous, the argument goes, places become less important (Meyrowitz 1985). But Harvey resists this line of argument:

> But it does not mean that the meaning of place has changed in social life and in certain respects the effect has been to make place more rather than less important. This probably accounts for the vast outpouring of works over the past ten years or so in which 'place' figures prominently in the title.
> (Harvey 1996, 297)

In conditions in which the global economy has reconfigured space and time radically, Harvey argues, people tend to think more about the security of their particular place in the world. The threat to place posed by the global economy makes us more aware of what we value in the places we live and work. In addition the dramatic reduction in costs of transport and communication, at least in the developed world, has made objective location (how far a place is from other places) less relevant. This means that the qualitative aspects of place – the quality of life – have increased in importance when a multinational company (for instance) chooses a location. Thus:

> Those who reside in a place ... become acutely aware that they are in competition with other places for highly mobile capital ... Residents worry about what package they can offer which will bring development while satisfying their own wants and needs. People in places therefore try to differentiate their place from other places and become more competitive (and perhaps antagonistic and exclusionary with respect to each other) in order to capture or retain capital investment. Within this process, the selling of place, using all the artifices of advertising and image construction that can be mustered has become of considerable importance.
>
> (Harvey 1996, 298)

Think of the efforts of cities around the world to become 'safe' and 'attractive' places for people to live and work. So called 'urban renaissance' projects such as the Guggenheim museum in Bilbao, Spain, the Millennium Dome in London or the Portman Center in downtown Atlanta are part and parcel of the need to attract both businesses and consumers (i.e. residents) to particular places rather than others. Similarly large cultural events such as World's Fairs, Olympic Games and World Cups are used to sell places to a world audience. Universities compete for students by advertising their location as well as their academic merit.

> Investment in consumption spectacles, the selling of images of places, competition over the definition of cultural and symbolic capital, the revival of vernacular traditions associated with places as a consumer attraction, all become conflated in inter-place competition.   (Harvey 1996, 298)

Harvey's next move is to consider the formative influence of the work of Martin Heidegger and his notion of 'dwelling'. He notes (as Edward Relph had several decades earlier) that Heidegger sees place-as-dwelling as the 'locale of the truth of being' – as the thing that makes humans human. He points out that Heidegger was already terrified of time-space compression in pre-war Germany because it resulted in a loss of place-based identity. It is this terror that forces Heidegger to withdraw from the world into his Black Forest farmhouse (see Chapter 2). Harvey finds this withdrawal problematic:

> For example, what might the conditions of 'dwelling' be in a highly industrialized, modernist, and capitalist world? We cannot turn back to the Black Forest farmhouse, but what is it that we might turn to? The issue of authenticity (rootedness) of the experience of place (and nature of place) is, for example a difficult one. To begin with ... the problem of authenticity is itself peculiarly modern. Only as modern industrialization separates us from the process of production and we encounter the environment as a finished commodity does it emerge. Being rooted in place, Tuan (1977, 198) argues, is a different kind of experience from having and cultivating a sense of place. 'A truly rooted community may have shrines and monuments, but it is unlikely to have museums and societies for the preservation of the past.' The effort to evoke a sense of place and of the past is now often deliberate and conscious.   (Harvey 1996, 302)

Clearly, then, it is not possible for large numbers of modern dwellers to retreat to farmhouses in the Black Forest or anywhere else (though where I live, in West Wales, there is plenty of evidence of people moving from the urban southeast of England to find some sense of attachment to place). But all around us there are efforts underway to make places more distinctive and visible and to provide a sense of pride and belonging. Often, as Harvey notes, this takes the form of 'heritage' where a sense of rootedness in the past and in place is provided for the consumption of locals and tourists. Urban areas are cleaned up and marketed as heritage areas (I am thinking of San Diego's gaslight district, London's Covent Garden or Boston's Faneuil Hall area). Signposts appear with elaborate 'olde worlde' maps and details of the history of this or that particular place. All of this is part of a search for 'authenticity' and rootedness. Ironically, of course, they are only necessary because 'being in place' cannot be taken for granted.

But the new values put on place are not simply for the benefit of tourists. Place has also become a political symbol for those who want to fight against the ever-present power of global capitalism. As Harvey notes, Kirkpatrick Sale was moved to write in *The Nation* that 'The only political vision that offers any hope of salvation is one based on an understanding of, a rootedness in, a deep commitment to, and a resacralization of *place*' (Harvey 1996, 302).

> This permits a second cut at why place is becoming more rather than less important in the contemporary world. What Heidegger holds out, and what many subsequent writers have drawn from him, is the possibility of some kind of resistance to or rejection of any simple capitalist (or modernist) logic of place construction. It would then follow that the increasing market penetration of technological rationality, of commodification and market values, and capital accumulation into social life ... together with time-space compression, will provoke resistances that increasingly focus on alternative constructions of place ... The search for an authentic sense of community and of an authentic relation to nature among many radical and ecological movements is the cutting edge of exactly such a sensibility.
>
> (Harvey 1996, 302)

This search for an authentic sense of place in the world is what Harvey (following Raymond Williams) calls 'militant particularism'. This term indicates the political use of the particularity of place as a form of resistance against the forces of global capitalism. All over the world groups have been and are attempting to build their own places and communities in order to live differently from the mass of people. Communes, organic farms, traveler communities, urban neighborhood groups and religious enclaves are all examples of this. Also, Harvey continues, place is often seen as the 'locus of collective memory' – a site where identity is created through the construction of memories linking a group of people into the past.

> The preservation or construction of a sense of place is then an active moment in the passage from memory to hope, from past to future. And the reconstruction of places can reveal hidden memories that hold out the prospects for different futures. 'Critical regionalism' as it is called in architecture, invoking as it so often does vernacular traditions and icons of place, is considered a basis for a politics of resistance to commodity flows and monetization. 'Militant particularism' seizes upon the qualities of place, reanimates the bond between the environmental and the social, and seeks to bend the social processes constructing space-time to a radically different purpose. Some memories can be suppressed and others rescued from the shadows as identities shift and political trajectories into the future get redefined ... Imagined places, the Utopian thoughts and desires of countless peoples, have consequently played a vital role in animating politics.
>
> (Harvey 1996, 306)

This construction of imagined places is important to Harvey (indeed he later wrote a whole book on the theme called *Spaces of Hope*

(Harvey 2000)). It is in these imagined places (sometimes partly realized as utopian communities) that people act out resistance to the wider world of capital accumulation. It is not just small groups of people leading alternative lifestyles that use place to resist the forces of global capital though. Mainstream religions and nations also need to use place to emphasize what they see as their distinctiveness and independence from wider pressures. Thus nations invest in monuments, grand buildings and other projects to fill the place of the nation with meaning and memory and thus secure their power and authority. In Britain the Labour government constructed the Millennium Dome in East London in order to produce a sense of national pride and project into the unknown future of the twenty-first century. In many respects this sense of investment in place shares much with the residents of Guilford seeking to protect and promote their little piece of Baltimore.

Harvey takes issue with the idea that a place can unproblematically stand for the memory and identity of a particular group of people. It may be true, he argues, that collective memory is often made concrete through the production of particular places but this production of memory in place is no more than an element in the perpetuation of a particular social order that seeks to inscribe some memories at the expense of others. Places do not come with some memories attached as it by nature but rather they are the 'contested terrain of competing definitions' (Harvey 1996, 309). He uses the example of the Acropolis in Athens. While some argue that the monument stands for a particular kind of Greece that is unique and separate from the rest of the world others insist that the place is the repository of a wider sense of 'Western civilization'.

> The burden that the Acropolis bears is that it simultaneously 'belongs' to radically divergent imagined communities. And the question as to whom it 'truly' belongs has no direct theoretical answer: it is determined through political contestation and struggle and, hence, is a relatively unstable determination.   (Harvey 1996, 310)

In summary then, Harvey portrays place as a deeply ambiguous facet of modern and postmodern life. On the one hand investments in place can play a role in resisting the global circulation of capital but on the other it is often quite an exclusionary force in the world where groups of people define themselves against threatening others who are not included in the particular vision of place being enacted. The flows of globalization, on the other hand, are seen as anxiety provoking for those people who seek to invest in the fixities of place-based existence.

Doreen Massey's paper is in many ways a response to this kind of thinking, a response that hinges on a redefinition of place as an inclusive and progressive site of social life. It appeared alongside Harvey's paper in the 1993 collection *Mapping the Futures*. Her paper is included, almost in its entirety below.

A Global Sense of Place

This is an era – it is often said – when things are speeding up, and spreading out. Capital is going through a new phase of internationalization, especially in its financial parts. More people travel more frequently and for longer distances. Your clothes have probably been made in a range of countries from Latin America to South East Asia. Dinner consists of food shipped in from all over the world. And if you have a screen in your office, instead of opening a letter which – care of Her Majesty's Post Office – has taken some days to wend its way across the country, you now get interrupted by e-mail.

This view of the current age is one now frequently found in a wide range of books and journals. Much of what is written about space, place and postmodern times emphasizes a new phase in what Marx once called 'the annihilation of space by time'. The process is argued, or – more usually – asserted, to have gained a new momentum, to have reached a new stage. It is a phenomenon which has been called 'time-space compression'. And the general acceptance that something of the sort is going on is marked by the almost obligatory use in the literature of terms and phrases such as speed-up, global village, overcoming spatial barriers, the disruption of horizons, and so forth.

One of the results of this is an increasing uncertainty about what we mean by 'places' and how we relate to them. How, in the face of all this movement and intermixing, can we retain any sense of a local place and its peculiarity? An (idealized) notion of an era when places were (supposedly) inhabited by coherent and homogeneous communities is set against the current fragmentation and disruption. The counterposition is anyway dubious, of course; 'place' and 'community' have only rarely been coterminous. But the occasional longing for such coherence is nonetheless a sign of the geographical fragmentation, the spatial disruption, of our times. And occasionally, too, it has been part of what has given rise to defensive and reactionary responses – certain forms of nationalism, sentimentalized recovering of sanitized 'heritages', and outright antagonism to newcomers and 'outsiders'. One of the effects of such responses is that place itself, the seeking after a sense of place, has come to be seen by some as necessarily reactionary.

But is that necessarily so? Can't we rethink our sense of place? Is it not possible for a sense of place to be progressive; not self-enclosing and defensive, but outward looking? A sense of place which is adequate to this era of time-space compression? To begin with, there are some questions to be asked about time-space compression itself. Who is it that experiences it and how? Do we all benefit from and suffer from it in the same way?

For instance, to what extent does the currently popular characterization of time-space compression represent very much a Western, colonizer's view? The sense of dislocation which some feel at the sight of a once well-known local street now lined with a succession of cultural imports – the pizzeria, the kebab house, the branch of the middle-eastern bank – must have been felt for centuries, though from a different point of view, by colonized peoples all over the world as they watched the importation, maybe even used, the products of, first, European colonization, maybe British (from new forms of transport to liver salts and custard powder), later US, as they learned to eat wheat instead of rice or corn, to drink Coca-Cola, just as today we try our enchiladas.

Moreover, as well as querying the ethnocentricity of the idea of time-space compression and its current acceleration, we also need to ask about its causes: what is it that determines our degrees of mobility, that influences the sense we have of space and place? Time-space compression refers to movement and communication across space, to the geographical stretching-out of social relations, and to our experience of all of this. The usual interpretation is that it results overwhelmingly from the actions of capital, and from its currently increasing internationalization. On this interpretation, then, it is time space and money which make the world go round, and us go round (or not) the world. It is capitalism and its developments which are argued to determine our understanding and our experience of space.

But surely this is insufficient. Among the many other things which clearly influence that experience, there are, for instance, 'race' and gender. The degree to which we can move between countries, or walk about the streets at night, or venture out of hotels in foreign cities, is not just influenced by 'capital'. Survey after survey has shown how women's mobility, for instance, is restricted – in a thousand different ways, from physical violence to being ogled at or made to feel quite simply 'out of place' – not by 'capital' but by men ... A simple resort to explanation in terms of 'money' or 'capital' alone could not begin to get to grips with the issue. The current speed-up may be strongly determined by economic forces, but it is not the economy alone which determines our experience of space and place. In other words, and put simply, there is a lot more determining how we experience space than what 'capital' gets up to.

...

Imagine for a moment that you are on a satellite, further out and beyond all actual satellites; you can see 'planet earth' from a distance and unusually for someone with only peaceful intentions, you are equipped with the kind of technology which allows you to see the colors of people's eyes and the numbers on their numberplates. You can see all the movement and tune in to all the communication that is going on. Furthest out are the satellites, then aeroplanes, the long haul between London and Tokyo and the hop from San Salvador to Guatemala City. Some of this is people moving, some of it is physical trade, some is media broadcasting. There are faxes, e-mails, film distribution networks, financial flows and transactions. Look in closer and there are ships and trains, steam trains slogging laboriously up hills somewhere in Asia. Look in closer still and there are lorries and cars and buses, and further down, somewhere in sub-Saharan Africa, there's a woman – amongst many women – on foot, who still spends hours a day collecting water.

Now I want to make one simple point here, and that is about what one might call the *power-geometry* of it all; the power geometry of time-space compression. For different social groups, and different individuals, are placed in very distinct ways in relation to these flows and interconnections. This point concerns not merely the issue of who moves and who doesn't, although that is an important element of it; it is also about power in relation *to* the flows and movement. Different social groups have distinct relationships to this anyway differentiated mobility: some people are more in charge of it than others; some initiate flows and movement, others don't; some are more on the receiving-end of it than others; some are effectively imprisoned by it.

In a sense at the end of all the spectra are those who are both doing the moving and the communicating and who are in some way in a position of control in relation to it – the jet-setters, the ones sending and receiving the faxes and the e-mail, holding the international conference calls, the ones distributing the films, controlling the news, organizing the investments and the international currency transactions. These are the groups who are really in a sense in charge of time-space compression, who can really use it and turn it to advantage, whose power and influence it very definitely increases. On its more prosaic fringes this group probably includes a fair number of Western academics and journalists – those, in other words, who write most about it.

But there are also groups who are also doing a lot of physical moving, but who are not 'in charge' of the process in the same way at all. The refugees from El Salvador and Guatemala and the undocumented migrant workers from Michoacán in Mexico, crowding into Tijuana to make a perhaps fatal dash for it across the border into the US to grab a chance of a new life. Here the experiences of movement, and indeed of a confusing plurality of cultures, is very different. And there are those from India, Pakistan, Bangladesh, the Caribbean, who come half way round the world only to get held up in an interrogation room at Heathrow.

Or – a different case again – there are those who are simply on the receiving end of time-space compression. The pensioner in a bed-sit in any inner city in the country, eating British working-class-style fish and chips from a Chinese take-away, watching a US film on a Japanese television; and

not daring to go out after dark. And anyway the public transport's been cut.
. . .
There is, in other words, a highly complex social differentiation. There are differences in the degree of movement and communication, but also in the degree of control and of initiation. The ways in which people are placed within 'time-space compression' are highly complicated and extremely varied.
. . .
But this way of thinking about time-space compression also returns us to the question of place and a sense of place. How, in the context of all these socially varied time-space changes do we think about 'places'? In an era when, it is argued, 'local communities' seem to be increasingly broken up, when you can go abroad and find the same shops, the same music as at home, or eat your favourite foreign-holiday food at a restaurant down the road – and when everybody has a different experience of all this – how do we think about 'locality'?

Many of those who write about time-space compression emphasize the insecurity and unsettling impact of its effects, the feelings of vulnerability which it can produce. Some, therefore go on from this to argue that, in the middle of all this flux, people desperately need a bit of peace and quiet – and that a strong sense of place, of locality, can form one kind of refuge from the hubbub. So the search after the 'real' meanings of place, the unearthing of heritages and so forth, is interpreted as being, in part, a response to desire for fixity and for security of identity in the middle of all the movement and change. A 'sense of place', of rootedness, can provide – in this form and on this interpretation – stability and a source of unproblematic identity. In that guise, however, place and the spatially local are then rejected by many progressive people as almost necessarily reactionary. They are interpreted as an evasion; as a retreat from the (actually unavoidable) dynamic and change of 'real life', which is what we must seize if we are to change things for the better. On this reading, place and locality are foci for a form of romanticized escapism from the real business of the world. While 'time' is equated with movement and progress, 'space/place' is equated with stasis and reaction.

There are some serious inadequacies in this argument. There is the question of why it is assumed that time-space compression will produce insecurity. There is the need to face up to – rather than simply deny – people's need for attachment of some sort, whether through place or anything else. Nonetheless, it is certainly the case that there is indeed at the moment a recrudescence of some very problematic senses of place, from reactionary nationalisms, to competitive localisms, to introverted obsessions with 'heritage'. We need, therefore, to think through what might be an adequately progressive sense of place, one which would fit in with the current global-local times and the feelings and relations they give rise to, *and*, which would be useful in what are, after all, political struggles often inevitably based on place. The question is how to hold on to that notion of geographical difference, of uniqueness, even of rootedness if people want that, without it being reactionary.

There are a number of distinct ways in which the 'reactionary' notion of place described above is problematic. One is the idea that places have single, essential, identities. Another is the idea that identity of place – the sense of place – is constructed out of an introverted, inward-looking history based on delving into the past for internalized origins, translating the name from the Domesday Book ... A particular problem with this conception of place is that it seems to require the drawing of boundaries. Geographers have long been exercised by the problem of defining regions, and this question of 'definition' has almost always been reduced to the issue of drawing lines around a place ... But that kind of boundary around an area precisely distinguishes between an inside and an outside. It can so easily be yet another way of constructing a counterposition between 'us' and 'them'.

And yet if one considers almost any real place, and certainly one not defined primarily by administrative or political boundaries, these supposed characteristics have little real purchase.

Take, for instance, a walk down Kilburn High Road, my local shopping centre. It is a pretty ordinary place, north-west of the centre of London. Under the railway bridge the newspaper stand sells papers from every county of what my neighbours, many of whom come from there, still often call the Irish Free State. The postboxes down the High Road, and many an empty space of a wall, are adorned with the letters IRA. Other available spaces are plastered this week with posters for a special meeting in remembrance: Ten Years after the Hunger Strike. At the local theatre Eamon Morrissey has a one-man show; the National Club has the Wolfe Tones on, and at the Black Lion there's Finnegan's Wake. In two shops I notice this week's lottery ticket winners: in one the name is Teresa Gleeson, in the other, Chouman Hassan.

Thread your way though the often almost stationary traffic diagonally across the road from the newsstand and there's a shop which as long as I can remember has displayed saris in the window. Four life-sized models of Indian women, and reams of cloth. On the door a notice announces a forthcoming concert at Wembley Arena: Anand Miland presents Rekha, live, with Aamir Khan, Jahi Chawla and Ravenna Tandon. On another ad, for the end of the month, is written, 'All Hindus are cordially invited'. In another newsagents I chat with the man who keeps it, a Muslim unutterably depressed by events in the Gulf, silently chafing at having to sell the *Sun*. Overhead there is always at least one aeroplane – we seem to be on a flight path to Heathrow and by the time they're over Kilburn you can see them clearly enough to tell the airline and wonder as you struggle with your shopping where they're coming from. Below, the reason the traffic is snarled up (another odd effect of time-space compression!) is in part because this is one of the main entrances to and escape routes from

London, the road to Staples Corner and the beginning of the M1 to 'the North'.

...

Kilburn is a place for which I have a great affection; I have lived there many years. It certainly has 'a character of its own'. But it is possible to feel all this without subscribing to any of the static and defensive – and in that sense reactionary – notions of 'place' which were referred to above. First, while Kilburn may have a character of its own, it is absolutely not a seamless, coherent identity, a single sense of place which everyone shares. It could hardly be less so. People's routes through the place, their favourite haunts within it, the connections they make (physically, or by phone or post, or in memory and imagination) between here and the rest of the world vary enormously. If it is now recognized that people have multiple identities then the same point can be made in relation to places. Moreover, such multiple identities can either be a source of richness or a source of conflict, or both.

One of the problems here has been a persistent identification of place with 'community'. Yet this is a misidentification. On the one hand, communities can exist without being in the same place – from networks of friends with like interests, to major religions, ethnic or political communities. On the other hand, the instances of places housing single 'communities' in the sense of coherent social groups are probably – and I would argue, have for long been – quite rare. Moreover, even where they do exist this in no way implies a single sense of place. For people occupy different positions within any community. We could counterpose to the chaotic mix of Kilburn the relatively stable and homogeneous community (at least of popular imagery) of a small mining village. Homogeneous? 'Communities' too have internal structures. To take the most obvious example, I'm sure a woman's sense of place in a mining village – the spaces through which she normally moves, the meeting places, the connections outside – are different from a man's. Their 'sense of place' will be different.

Moreover, not only does 'Kilburn', then, have many different identities (or its full identity is a complex mix of all these) it is also, looked at in this way, absolutely *not* introverted. It is (or ought to be) impossible even to begin thinking about Kilburn High Road without bringing into play half the world and a considerable amount of British imperialist history (and this certainly goes for mining villages too). Imagining it this way provokes in you (or at least in me) a really global sense of place.

And finally, in contrasting this way of looking at places with the defensive, reactionary view, I certainly could not begin to, nor would I want to, define 'Kilburn' by drawing its enclosing boundaries.

So, at this point in the argument, get back in your mind's eye on a satellite; go right out again and look back at the globe. This time, however, imagine not just all the physical movement, nor even all the often invisible communications, but also and especially all the social relations, all the links between people. Fill it in with all those different experiences of time-space compression. For what is happening is that the geography of social relations is changing. In many cases such relations are increasingly stretched out over space. Economic, political and cultural social relations, each full of power and with internal structures of domination and subordination, stretched out over the planet at every different level, from the household to the local area to the international.

It is from that perspective that it is possible to envisage an alternative interpretation of place. In this interpretation, what gives a place its specificity is not some long internalized history but the fact that it is constructed out of a particular constellation of social relations, meeting and weaving together at a particular locus. If one moves in from the satellite towards the globe, holding all those networks of social relations and movements and communications in one's head, then each 'place' can be seen as a particular, unique, point of their intersection. It is, indeed, a *meeting* place. Instead then, of thinking of places as areas with boundaries around, they can be imagined as articulated moments in networks of social relations and understandings, but where a large proportion of those relations, experiences and understandings are constructed on a far larger scale than what we happen to define for that moment as the place itself, whether that be a street, or a region or even a continent. And this in turn allows a sense of place which is extroverted, which includes a consciousness of its links with the wider world, which integrates in a positive way the global and the local.

This is not a question of making the ritualistic connections to 'the wider system' – the people in the local meeting who bring up international capitalism every time you try and have a discussion about rubbish-collection – the point is that there are real relations with real content – economic, political, cultural – between any local place and the wider world in which it is set. In economic geography the argument has long been accepted that it is not possible to understand the 'inner city', for instance its loss of jobs, the decline of manufacturing employment there, by looking only at the inner city. Any adequate explanation has to set the inner city in its wider geographical context. Perhaps it is appropriate to think how that kind of understanding could be extended to the notion of sense of place.

These arguments, then, highlight a number of ways in which a progressive concept of place might be developed. First of all, it is absolutely not static. If places can be conceptualized in terms of the social interactions which they tie together, then it is also the case that these interactions themselves are not motionless things, frozen in time. They are processes. One of the great one-liners of Marxist exchanges has for long been, 'Ah, but capital is not a thing, it is a process.' Perhaps this should be said also about places; that places are processes, too.

Second, places do not have to have boundaries in the sense of divisions which frame simple enclosures. 'Boundaries' may of course be necessary, for the purposes of certain kinds of studies for instance, but they are not necessary for the conceptualization of a place itself. Definition in this sense does not have be through simple counterposition to the outside; it can come, in part, precisely through the particularity of linkage *to* that 'outside' which is therefore itself part of what constitutes the place. This helps us get away from the common association between penetrability and vulnerability. For it is this kind of association which makes invasion by newcomers so threatening.

Third, clearly places do not have single, unique 'identities'; they are full of internal conflicts. Just think, for instance, about London's Docklands, a place which is at the moment quite clearly *defined* by conflict: a conflict over what its past has been (the nature of its 'heritage'), conflict over what should be its present development, conflict over what should be its future.

Fourth, and finally, none of this denies place nor the importance of the uniqueness of place. The specificity of place is continually reproduced, but it is not a specificity which results from some long, internalized history. There are a number of sources of this specificity – the uniqueness of place. There is the fact that the wider social relations in which places are set are themselves geographically differentiated. Globalization (in the economy, or in culture, or in anything else) does not entail simply homogenization. On the contrary, the globalization of social relations is yet another source of (the reproduction of) geographical uneven development, and thus of the uniqueness of place. There is the specificity of place which derives from the fact that each place is the focus of a distinct *mixture* of wider and more local social relations. There is the fact that this very mixture together in one place may produce effects which would not have happened otherwise. And finally, all these relations interact with and take a further element of specificity from the accumulated history of a place, with that history itself imagined as the product of layer upon layer of different sets of linkages, both local and to the wider world.

In her portrait of Corsica, *Granite Island*, Dorothy Carrington travels the island seeking out the roots of its character. All the different layers of peoples and cultures are explored; the long and tumultuous relationship with France, with Genoa and Aragon in the thirteenth, fourteenth and fifteenth centuries, back though the much earlier incorporation into the Byzantine Empire, and before that domination by the Vandals, before that being part of the Roman Empire, before that the colonization and settlements of the Carthaginians and the Greeks ... until we find ... that even the megalith builders had come to Corsica from somewhere else.

It is a sense of place, an understanding to 'its character' which can only be constructed by linking that place to places beyond. A progressive sense of place would recognize that, without being threatened by it. What we need, its seems to me, is a global sense of local, a global sense of place.

Massey's first move in this paper is to question dominant assumptions about time-space compression and globalization. As we saw in Harvey's paper these global flows of people, information, products and capital are often seen as anxiety provoking – as forces to be resisted. Massey's view is different. She argues that such views are the product of seeing global processes purely in terms of capitalism. And yet, she points out, they are also gendered and raced. The ubiquitous mobility of the world is too often portrayed as a universal condition resulting from transformations in capital. Harvey may agree that mobilities are often differentiated according to race and gender but these are not the aspects he emphasizes. Massey uses examples of people moving in all kinds of ways to show how the reasons for people's movements are far from homogeneous. Some are forced to move, some move at will and others are effectively forced to stay still. To simply pit the apparent fixity of place against the apparent fluidity of the global economy, Massey suggests, is to miss the specificity of people's mobile experience.

Massey gives many examples of this which are easy to relate to and we can all think of others. Take, for example, the relationship between the global elite, the 'ex-pats' for instance, who live in Hong Kong or Singapore and the people that serve them – the domestic servants from the Philippines or the cleaners and maids who look after their rooms in Hyatts and Marriots all over the world. They are all mobile but in very different ways and for different reasons. To think of them all as simply fragments of the globalization of capital misses the point. There are clear issues of gender and race in these examples too. Cleaners and maids in business class hotels in the developed West are usually poorer migrant women from the less developed world. The people in the rooms are from different worlds. Hong Kong's ex-pat community is wealthy and predominantly white and male. The domestic servants are not. Massey uses the phrase 'power-geometry' to describe the way in which the complicated movements of people are infused with power that is not only an issue of capital but also other ubiquitous forms of social relation.

Massey's next move is to suggest that when we rethink 'time-space compression' and 'globalization' in these ways we also have to think again about place. She notes how one response to time-space compression has been the sense of anxiety that leads to people looking for a 'little peace and quiet' and retreating into a romantic sense of place very much like the one outlined by Harvey. Such a retreat, Massey points out, is almost necessarily reactionary. She cites nationalisms, heritage crusades and the fear of outsiders as examples of reactionary withdrawals into place. All of these were very apparent in the early 1990s when she was writing. Now we could think of the almost pathological hatred of 'asylum seekers' in the United Kingdom, the more generalized fear of the foreign in post 9/11 USA and the treatment of potential Afghan immigrants to Australia as examples of the same kind of retreat.

And yet to simply see place as a static and rooted reaction to a dynamic and mobile world holds several problems for Massey. First it may be the case that people do need some sense of place to hold on to – even a need for 'rootedness' – and this need not be always reactionary. Second the flow and flux of global movement might not necessarily be anxiety provoking. The reactionary sense of place that disturbs Harvey is, for Massey marked by at least three interconnected ways of thinking.

1. A close connection between place and a singular form of identity.
2. A desire to show how the place is authentically rooted in history.
3. A need for a clear sense of boundaries around a place separating it from the world outside.

The first of these suggests that particular places have singular unitary identities – New York means this, Wales means that. Often these identities are based on ideas about race. Place at the national scale for instance often acts in a way that ties a particular 'race' or ethnic group to a particular area of land. So the ex-British Prime Minister John Major famously argued that Britain was a nation of 'long shadows on county cricket grounds, warm beer, invincible green suburbs, dog lovers and – as George Orwell said – old maids bicycling to Holy Communion through the morning mist.' Clearly this is not everyone's view of Britain. The idea that particular groups of people with their own 'culture' belong, as if by nature, in a particular place is, however, widespread. Successive America presidents have made similar statements about the United States. Ronald Reagan in September 1980 said in a televised debate:

> I have always believed that this land was placed here between the two great oceans by some divine plan. It was placed here to be found by a special kind of people – people who had a special love for freedom and who had the courage to uproot themselves and leave hearth and homeland and come to what in the beginning was the most undeveloped wilderness possible. We spoke a multitude of tongues – landed on this eastern shore and then went out over the mountains and the prairies and the deserts and the far Western mountains of the Pacific, building cities and towns and farms and schools and churches.

Just as Major tapped into well-developed stereotypes about Britain as a particular kind of place so Reagan mobilized long-held views of 'America' as a frontier nation for particular political ends. There is almost a common-sense way in which particular identities are mapped onto the world. We will see in Chapter 4 how such visions often lead to reprehensible treatment of those who do not fit such an identity.

The second part of Massey's delineation of a reactionary sense of place is the constant desire to show how places and their identities are rooted in history. This explains the modern desire for heritage at both national and local scales. National governments and cultural elites are often keen to root a sense of national identity in a historical story of where it has come from and where it is going – a creation myth. Elaborate traditions are invented in order to bolster these stories. Museums display these histories. Not far from where I live and work there is a museum called Celtica which taps into colorful myths about the Celts – the semi-mythical body of people who are supposed to provide the deep-rooted historical heritage of Wales (as well as Scotland, Ireland, Brittany, etc.). This is far from unique and places like it, can, I imagine, be found just about all over the globe. Often these histories are very selective and exclude the experiences of more recent arrivals. Returning to the idea of 'Britishness' the conservative politician Norman Tebbit made the following claim in September 2002: 'My father's family came to Britain in the 16th Century, but I regard the Anglo-Saxon period, King Alfred and William the Conqueror as part of my inheritance.' He went on to say how the challenge for late twentieth century Britain was, as he saw it to: 'persuade these people (immigrants) that Waterloo, Trafalgar and the Battle of Britain, is part of their heritage.' Here a particular exclusionary view of heritage is mapped onto a place – Britain – in a way that effectively excludes a large portion of the British population for whom other aspects of British history – colonialism, slavery, economic exploitation – may be more immediate.

The third issue in the reactionary definition of place is that of boundaries. Boundaries are a key element in Massey's discussion. She makes it quite clear that, to her, places are not about boundaries. Boundaries, she argues, simply make distinctions between 'them' and 'us' and therefore contribute to a reactionary politics. This, of course, stands in distinction to Harvey's tale of Guilford and the construction of very literal boundaries in the form of walls and gates around it. Of course some places have literal boundaries and others do not. Nation-states have boundaries which have to be negotiated. Political entities within nations also have formal boundaries that we often cross without noticing. On a smaller scale, however, we are often hard pressed to think of where a place begins and ends. And focusing on this issue, as Massey points out, tends to negate the multitude of flows that cross boundaries constantly. Massey's criticism here, however, is a little misplaced as very few geographers (outside of those dealing with the geopolitics of national and sub-national boundaries) write about boundaries in relation to place. Humanists, for instance, would be the last to claim that place was clearly and unambiguously bounded.

Massey's description of Kilburn is a celebration of diversity and hybridity. Her portrait is an evocative mix of people of multiple ethnicities living and working side by side. The symbols she picks out are symbols of Irish, Muslim or Hindu life. This is quite clearly not a place seeking to distance itself from the wide world but one made up of constantly changing elements of that wider world. Massey's Kilburn is, in her words, a 'meeting place' where a particular 'constellation of social relations' comes together in place. Her observations of Kilburn draws her toward a new 'extrovert' 'progressive' and 'global' sense of place marked by the following:

1. Place as process.
2. Place as defined by the outside.
3. Place as site of multiple identities and histories.
4. A uniqueness of place defined by its interactions.

Massey's new definition of place is really quite different from ones that went before it. Tuan and Relph, you will recall, were quite clear that processes and forms of movement were, when extended too far, quite antithetical to the construction of places. The French anthropologist Marc Augé also sees travel as the moving force in the construction of non-place. So what would these writers on place make of Massey's use of the word? One criticism that it is possible to make of the 'global sense of place' is that it is hard to point to anything specific about it. The traditional humanistic definition of place at least has the advantage of being quite clear about the importance of the existential sense of rootedness to make their arguments for the importance of place. What is the 'place' component of Massey's Kilburn? Is it no more than an accidental coming together of many different flows in one location?

And surely it is also the case that many people all over the world do invest (in non-reactionary ways) in a search for comparative fixity. Although it is true that there are few places not influenced by global flows of commodities, ideas and people there are many places where families have lived for generations or where a little more globalization would be welcome. I am thinking here of towns where locals would like a local branch of a global chain such as Starbucks, McDonalds or the Body Shop but the local economy is simply too marginal and depressed for these symbols of the globe to locate there. In Chapter 4 we will see how some groups make quite positive and inclusive attempts to tap into a place's history or promote a particular notion of place as an act of resistance and affirmation in the face of wider forces. In other words, a little bit of fixity might not always be such a bad thing.

A great deal, it seems to me, depends on what particular instance of place we chose to look at. Both Harvey and Massey choose to illustrate their ideas about place with reference to specific places near to where they live – Harvey writes about Guilford in Baltimore and Massey considers Kilburn in London. Both of these places obviously mean something to the authors personally. But notice how different the examples are. Harvey's Guilford is a place that sees itself under threat from difference and seeks to create clear boundaries – literally a wall with monitored gates – to distinguish itself from the threatening outside. Massey's Kilburn on the other hand is a place of radical openness – defined by its permeability. It is not surprising, therefore, that the more theoretical considerations of place that follow are different too. To Harvey place seems just too reactionary – too based on the exclusion of 'others'. Massey's Kilburn, on the other hand allows her to suggest that it is okay to seek identity in place because the identity is never fixed and bounded.

Beyond Reactionary and Progressive Senses of Place

Stoke Newington is an area of Inner North London which has recently been subject to gentrification. A new cultural elite has moved in along with their expensive and diverse restaurants, boutiques and furniture shops.

> If we are to believe the pundits, Stoke Newington has arrived. Take a stroll through Church Street, the trendier of the area's two shopping centers, and the suspicion is confirmed. In place of the old barbers there is now a kite shop, instead of a butchers, a delicatessen. The fish and chip shop has long gone, replaced by a (reassuringly expensive) Indian restaurant and in its book shops one no longer need to search through Frederick Forsyth to find the elusive little collection on Forster. (May 1996, 197)

Jon May conducted his doctoral research there and found that the politics of place in Stoke Newington should lead us to be careful about putting all our eggs in one theoretical basket in regards to place. His research involved ethnographic fieldwork and extensive interviewing of local residents – both working class and members of the new cultural elite. One couple, Paul and Pat, look back to the 'good old days' of Stoke Newington as a cohesive working class (and white) neighborhood where everyone knew each other and you didn't have to lock the door. For them the main reason the place has changed for the worse is immigration. They blame immigrants (i.e. non-white people) for crime and decay of community.

> Jon: Because it must have been, when you were little, it must have been almost entirely white around here.
>
> Pat: Oh yeah, yeah! Yeah it was. And you left your front door open all night and it wouldn't matter. You know, it just wouldn't matter. But now! God, you got to lock everything up.   (May 1996, 200)

To Pat and Paul, Stoke Newington is not a place of new and appealing diversity but a place in decline (Paul has suffered from a declining local job market and has had seven jobs in ten years – many part time). Paul looks at the 'diversity' of the area and sees scapegoats for his own precarious situation. Pat and Paul's sense of loss, although clearly racist, is nonetheless profound.

> Both Paul and Pat have seen the area where they grew up change beyond all recognition and such changes precipitate a very real sense of loss. For Pat, this sense of disenfranchisement has become centered upon the High Street where those landmarks through which she has always constructed her sense of place are being appropriated by others and where, when she feels as if she has nowhere to go, it seems as though others are being provided with a readymade sense of place.   (May 1996, 201)

Despite the despair of Pat and Paul over the rising immigrant (principally Kurdish) population and diminished sense of English-ness, others are attracted to the area because it does 'conjure up images of this England lost; a quieter more stable England of parish churches and village greens, reaching back to the area's founding moment as the "village in the woode"' (May 1996, 202). The local council installed mock gas lamps along one street while residents were busy installing wood floors and Aga cookers. Two streets (Shakespeare Walk and Milton Grove) were granted conservation status in order to promote the heritage of the area. May interviewed a graphic designer (Alex) who had recently moved into the area because of the iconography of Englishness. Note how different Alex's perspective is from Pat and Paul's:

> Coming from Church Street you've got that glorious shot of the church spires and trees and the park, and all that ... it's a real sort of postcardy thing. The only that that's missing is the cricket pitch ... It's very sort of Englishy, and I think it will probably remain so, you know.
>
> Alex quoted by (May 1996, 203)

So Alex sees Stoke Newington almost as a picture of stereotypical Englishness while Paul and Pat see only a lack of the very same qualities. Alex's vision is similarly based on racial homogeneity. Neither of these visions of the place could be said to be progressive. Both look to the past for a sense of Englishness but they are very different visions. Paul and Pat look to a past that is working class based on High Street pubs and corner stores while Alex buys into the (middle class) iconography of churches and rurality. This is best illustrated by their differing accounts of a local pub that had been called the Red Lion and had been changed to the Magpie and Stump. To Alex the change of name and the redecorated interior marked a distinct improvement – it became a comfortable middle class establishment that Alex referred to as 'traditional'. Before the change the pub had been, in Alex's eyes 'an awful place with about three people in there'. To Paul, however, this change was just another sign of the erosion of the place he had known. The Red Lion had been a place Paul had grown up going to and playing darts in. The Magpie and Stump was now a yuppie pub: 'It used to be a nice pub, and I mean the Red Lion, it's a nice name for a pub. The Magpie and Stump! Why bring in the yuppy names, why not keep the traditional thing?!' (May 1996, 203). As May puts it:

> Battles over an area's past are therefore of crucial importance in defining a local sense of place. But at issue is not some elusive question of historical authenticity, of whose image of the past is closer to what an area was 'really like'. Rather, it is a question of the material politics articulated by each vision. Ironically, that sense of Englishness – constructed through a particular reading of the area's past – that Stoke Newington's middle class residents are building, is directly contributing to that sense of England lost that pervaded Paul and Pat's earlier accounts and complicating any ideas of a universal retreat into the mythology of a 'bounded' sense of place.   (May 1996, 205)

Beyond the senses of place of Pat and Paul on the one hand and Alex on the other, May found another way of thinking about Stoke Newington that gestured toward Massey's global sense of place. Some residents were attracted to Stoke Newington *because* of its perceived diversity. Amanda is another resident of the area who takes pleasure in the sights and sounds of a local market place.

> It's just that I LEARN things there, I mean its really humbling sometimes ... for instance, there's a lot of Africans and West Indians that I talk to, colleagues and friends at work – more Africans – who really sneer at us because we are the so called 'civilised society', but we've lost a big part of ourselves. Whether it's a spiritual part, or a bit that you can't really, you know, it's not logical, it's not material, and that's really quite recent for me.
> Amanda in (May 1996, 206)

To May, people such as Amanda enjoy a kind of aestheticized difference – they stand back from the crowd and enjoy it in all its variety. May argues that this is an appreciation of diversity as a picturesque scene that gives those who look on a sense of cultural capital – a sense of their own self worth in being able to appreciate difference. For Amanda and others 'the city and its other residents are reduced to the sights of an afternoon stroll, part of an agreeable lifestyle aesthetic for those suitably insulated from the reality of life in a declining inner-city neighbourhood' (May 1996, 208)

Crucially this sense of an aesthetic appreciation of difference cannot be reconciled with either Harvey's or Massey's sense of place:

> [T]he images of Stoke Newington provided by some of the area's new cultural class residents suggest neither that radically 'bounded' sense of place identified by some ... nor yet the emergence of that more 'progressive' sense of place championed by others ... Rather, it has been suggested that we may need to recognize the multiple place identities people now draw upon and consider more carefully the ways in which such identities are constructed. The control over local space which Stoke Newington's new cultural class residents now enjoy, for example, allows such residents to construct Stoke Newington as a space in which 'one can have it all'. Whilst the neighbourhood's historical associations can support an image of place built around the iconography of a mythical village England, those same residents demonstrate a desire for difference that draws them towards a more obviously 'global sense of place'. Yet the way in which this latter place identity is constructed is anything but progressive, suggesting we may need to pay more attention to the way in which such connections are imagined,

and by whom, before automatically assuming that a global sense of place describes a more progressive identity politics.   (May 1996, 210–211)

May's engagement with Stoke Newington and its residents provides a third example of the politics of place in a globalized world. Unlike the essays of Harvey and Massey, May's paper is based on several years of ethnographic fieldwork to find out the multiple ways in which people relate to the same place. Issues of boundaries and rootedness and connections are still there but they are used in complicated ways by people. The simple, observable, fact of diversity does not necessarily produce a progressive sense of place and the search for roots in history does not have to be reactionary.

Conclusions

These accounts of place, through the examples of Guilford, Kilburn and Stoke Newington, reveal just how complicated the idea of place is. It is not just that these are different places in the simple sense of being located in different parts of London and in Baltimore. They all have complicated relationships both to the past and to other places near and far. But these accounts also show how place is a way of understanding the world. The theorizations of place by Massey, Harvey and May lead them to see different aspects of these places in the world. But theory is not just the property of intellectuals. Paul and Pat, Alex and Amanda, the residents of Stoke Newington, are also everyday theorists who bring their own ideas of place to bear of the place they live in. As with Massey, Harvey and May they understand place differently.

4

Working with Place

So far this book has dealt with the conceptual problems of thinking about place through the history of human geography. Chapter 2 considered the history of the concept of place in human geography and beyond while Chapter 3 looked at recent debates about the nature of place in the face of globalization. This chapter considers the way the concept of place has been and can be used in research. Because place is such a broad concept this is a potentially endless task. In some way or another the majority of geographical research is about place. As we have seen, many geographers define the discipline as the study of place. This chapter, however, considers work that uses place as an analytical concept that involves the process of shaping meaning and practice in material space. Research on place in this sense is necessarily concerned with how these meanings and practices are produced and consumed. With that in mind the first half of this chapter considers research on the creation of meanings in place. The second half considers how practices that do not conform to the expectations of place are labeled 'out-of-place' and thus how place is implicated in the construction of 'moral geographies.'

Thinking about and with place cannot easily be separated into 'theory and practice'. So although this chapter is looking at the way place has been used in empirical research that does not mean it is not also about theoretical attitudes to place. The particular research projects on place that people select are very dependent on what view of place they take at a theoretical level. This chapter, then, provides an additional opportunity to revisit some of the debates in earlier chapters.

Creating Places

The first part of this chapter is about the production of place. But it is important to remember that places are not like shoes or automobiles – they do not come out of a factory as finished products. Places, as Pred, Massey and others have reminded us in earlier chapters, are very much in process. Clearly places are created by cultural practices such as literature, film and music and the investigation of these forms of producing places are a central strand in contemporary human geography (Burgess and Gold 1985; Cresswell and Dixon 2002; Leyshon *et al.* 1998; Aitken and Zonn 1994). But most places are more often the product of everyday practices. Places are never finished but produced through the reiteration of practices – the repetition of seemingly mundane activities on a daily basis. As we have seen, the contemporary fascination with processes of flow and mobility in a globalized world often posits the end of place and the arrival of non-place. And yet place, even relatively fixed and bounded kinds of place, remains important. Even the United States, a place marked by an ideology of constant movement, is a nation where only eight per cent of people possess passports. Small towns in Arkansas or even urban neighborhoods of London can be marked by considerable immobility. People are creating places at all scales and everywhere in a myriad of different ways. This section is divided into four sets of examples of ways in which the creation of place has been considered in recent research. The first concerns the continued importance of place in a mobile and globalized world at the scale of the room and the region, the second focuses on the production of places of memory, the third looks at the production of place-identities for places to live and the final considers the creation of place at the larger scales of the region and the nation-state.

Creating place in a mobile world

Geraldine Pratt, a Canadian geographer, has been looking at the lives of Filipina contract workers in Vancouver. She tells the story of one woman called Mhay. Mhay used a room in the house of her employers to make herself visible.

> I bought a picture with a frame and put it on the wall. Prior to this, all four walls were bare. I did this without telling them because I thought that since I paid for this room, I should be allowed to do something about it. So I arranged the room, put furniture and TV [the way I wanted them]. I would

leave the door open so that they [my employers] could see what's in my
room, that it's not dull anymore.   (Quoted in Pratt 1999, 152)

Pratt pulls apart this observation in the context of feminist analysis of
the notion of 'home' and post-structural theorizations of hybrid
identity. She traces the feminist critique of the cosy idea of home
celebrated by Tuan in his notion of place as home. Home, as we have
seen, has been the object of deep distrust by feminists such as Rose
(1993) and de Lauretis (1990). The image of home as a peaceful and
meaningful refuge has been described as masculinist – hiding the
realities of power relations in the home which, at their extreme, are
linked to battery and rape. In place of home some have argued that, in
Massey's words, 'One gender-disturbing message might be – in terms
of both identity and space – keep moving!' (Massey 1994, 11). This is
not Pratt's point though. She argues that it is much easier to make
theory-level statements about home from the position of someone
who has a secure one. Mhay, the Filipina domestic worker, in contrast,
has a rather fragile claim to home as a domestic worker admitted into
Canada on a special visa. Mhay lives a paradoxical existence of
mobility and confinement with only the barest control over her own
space – the little things that make space into place, such as a poster on
a wall, get heightened significance. Pratt asks us to consider the role of
place construction and boundary maintenance in the construction of
identities.

> It seems to me that it is by starkly outlining the boundaries that separate my
> life from that of Mhay, by unravelling the layers of social-material borders
> that both produce and hem in our movements and identities, that a basis for
> communication and collaboration can be established. Marking boundaries,
> insisting on the materiality and persistence of differences, may be as
> politically productive as blurring them in notions of mobility, hybridity and
> thirdspace.   (Pratt 1999, 164)

Pratt's observation is clearly a critique of the emphasis on the mobile
and the hybrid in contemporary theory – pointing out that place and
boundary still do matter even in the world of a migrant worker.
Research on the place-making strategies of relatively powerless
people at a micro-level is an effective use of the idea of place. Here
Pratt's research with domestic workers raises some important
questions about the kind of open and fluid place described and
advocated by Massey (1997).

    The second example comes from Arturo Escobar. He is concerned
with the hegemonic global currency of the term 'globalization' and

the way in which a focus on global processes in the realm of space can be brought into question by a renewed interest in place and the local.

> Subaltern strategies of localization still need to be seen in terms of place; places are surely connected and constructed yet those constructions entail boundaries, grounds, selective connection, interaction and positioning, and in some cases a renewel of history-making skills.   (Escobar 2001, 169)

Just as Pratt was keen to show how Mhay was able to engage in place-construction in a context of relative powerlessness so Escobar argues that indigenous rainforest communities are able to construct places at a much larger scale. On one level this is a theoretical debate about the scale of enquiry necessary to understand power and the lifeworld. On another level it is a political project. In a world where forms of globalization associated with multinational flexible capitalism prevail and appear to flatten out difference – not least in the form of the development requirements of the World Bank and IMF – maybe a renewed focus on place formation can provide a basis for subaltern strategies of 'localization.' Escobar shows how new social movements, particularly in Latin America, are 'getting back into place.' His examples revolve around the black communities of Colombian Pacific rainforest. Activists of the Process of Black Communities (PCN) have articulated a complicated set of place-based identities in the face of the forces of globalization. Briefly put, strategies of globalization under-taken by the state, capital and technoscience all attempt to negotiate the production of locality in a non place-based way that induces increasingly delocalizing effects. In other words top-down globaliza-tion is insensitive to the specificity of place. Global capital does not care about the specificities of areas of the Colombian rainforest – or anywhere else for that matter. Meanwhile the strategies of localisation undertaken by social movements rely on attachments to territory and culture and ecology. Simultaneously they activate global networks (in the United Nations for instance) around the issue of biodiversity which act to reaffirm the importance of local particularity. This is achieved through an emphasis on the uniqueness of local production systems in unique ecological zones geared to local markets rather than the demands of global capital. The production of a particular kind of nut which is unique to a particular place is one example. A key part of this is the construction of a 'cultural ecology' of place. The region Escobar writes about is called the 'Pacífico biogeográfico' and a large part of the place-making strategy used by activists rests on its unique biological resources. But the Process of Black Communities cannot simply produce and defend place on this basis. Paradoxically in order for localization to occur the place has to project itself onto the global scale of capital and modernity. This is not simply the substitution of place-based authenticity for global appropriation but a recognition that place can play a strategic role in a world of hypermobility. Theoretically, Escobar writes:

> It is important to learn to see place-based cultural, ecological, and economic practices as important sources of alternative visions and strategies for reconstructing local and regional worlds, no matter how produced by 'the global' they might also be. Socially, it is necessary to think about the conditions that might make the defence of place – or, more precisely, of particular constructions of place and the reorganisation of place this might entail – a realizable project. (Escobar 2001, 165–166)

Both Pratt and Escobar, through their very different examples, show how a new focus on place might simultaneously bring into question the widely held belief that places, boundaries and rootedness are always necessarily either reactionary or a thing of the past. Pratt's domestic workers and Escobar's Colombian activists are both creating places from positions of comparative weakness in order to nullify the negative effects of globalization.

Place and memory

We have already seen how an important part of the creation of a sense of place is through a focus on particular and selective aspects of history. Notions of memory and heritage were right at the center of the debates in Chapter 3. Place and memory are, it seems, inevitably intertwined. Memory appears to be a personal thing – we remember some things and forget others. But memory is also social. Some memories are allowed to fade – are not given any kind of support. Other memories are promoted as standing for this and that. One of the primary ways in which memories are constituted is through the production of places. Monuments, museums, the preservation of particular buildings (and not others), plaques, inscriptions and the promotion of whole urban neighborhoods as 'heritage zones' are all examples of the placing of memory. The very materiality of a place means that memory is not abandoned to the vagaries of mental processes and is instead inscribed in the landscape – as public memory.

> If place does provide an overload of possible meanings for the researcher, it is place's very same assault on all ways of knowing (sight, sound, smell, touch and taste) that makes it powerful as a source of memory, as a weave

where one strand ties in another. Place needs to be at the heart of urban
landscape history, not on the margins.   (Hayden 1995, 18)

It is, as Delores Hayden suggests, the very complicated nature of the
experience of place that makes it an effective tool in the (re)production
of memory. It is one thing to read about the past in the book or see it
displayed in a painting – it is quite another to enter the realm of
history-in-place. A similar point in made by Edward Casey when he
writes of 'place memory'.

It is the stabilizing persistence of place as a container of experiences that
contributes so powerfully to its intrinsic memorability. An alert and alive
memory connects spontaneously with place, finding in it features that favor
and parallel its own activities. We might even say that memory if naturally
place-oriented or at least place-supported.   (Casey 1987, 186–187)

Recall that in New York's Lower East Side there is an area known as
the Tenement District. It is here that poor immigrants often found
their first home in one of the city's notorious tenements – buildings
with very little light packed with small living spaces often shared by
large families. If you visit there now you will find the Lower East Side
Tenement Museum – a preserved tenement with rooms arranged to
demonstrate how they would have looked at different points in the
building's history. It is an impressive place of memory because
something of what it might have been like to live in these places is
successfully recreated. The rooms are small, dark and uncomfortable
but full of items that were used over a hundred years earlier. Hayden
reflects on just such an experience:

In a typical New York tenement at the turn of the century, many people's
sordid habitat was one landlord's money machine, generating 25 percent
return on investment per year. There were few reasons to diminish profits
through maintenance expenses, since legal enforcement of building codes
and safety regulations was minimal. What did it mean in terms of the
sensory experience of place? The building will be a more evocative source
than any written records. One can read about unhealthy living conditions,
but standing inside a tenement apartment – perhaps 400 square feet of
living space for an entire family, minimal plumbing, only one or two
exterior windows – leaves a visitor gasping for air and looking for light. The
claustrophobic experiences of immigrants living for decades in crowded,
unhealthy space (as part of the reproduction of the labor force) are
conveyed by the building in a way that a text or chart can never match.
                                                         (Hayden 1995, 33-4)

This is what Casey means by place–memory – the ability of place to make the past come to life in the present and thus contribute to the production and reproduction of social memory. The Lower East Side Tenement Museum is something of a rarity, however, in that it seeks to inscribe in place the memory of groups of people at the bottom of a social hierarchy. For the most part places of memory serve to commemorate the winners of history. Endless state capitols, museums and public monuments in cities around the world make sure that a particular view of history is remembered – one of heroes on horseback. In many ways the Lower East Side Tenement Museum stands in contrast to a monument such as the Statue of Liberty which is often used to represent an official set of memories of the United States as a welcoming place for immigrants. Likewise the nearby Ellis Island Immigration Museum portrays a largely positive account of American immigration as a story of success and opportunity. It includes, for instance, a 'wall of honor' on which people can pay one hundred dollars to have their immigrant ancestors inscribed on a wall. It is only recently that places have been designated as sites of memory for women, black people, the poor and dispossessed. Just as the inhabitants of a place like Guilford in Baltimore literally seek to exclude those beyond, so places of memory also enact an exclusion, literal and figurative, of those memories that are painful or shameful.

Andrew Charlesworth (1994) has examined the role of the Nazi concentration camp, Auschwitz, Poland, as a place of memory. His paper focuses on the way the place and the memories associated with it have been contested. More specifically he argues that there has been a concerted attempt to 'Catholicize' Auschwitz from the 1970s onwards – a process that has sought to exclude and marginalize specifically Jewish memories of the place as a site of genocide. Before and during World War II, four million people perished in Auschwitz. Eighty-seven per cent of these victims were Jewish. A third of these were Polish Jews. Auschwitz was selected as a place of memory by the Soviet-backed communist regime in Poland following the war. It suited their purposes well as it could be portrayed solely as a symbol of fascist aggression. Jews from many nations had been killed there and this international aspect of the genocide meant that the government could effectively ignore the fact that the victims were Jewish and instead memorialize their international origins. The site became a place where Western aggression against the nations of Eastern Europe could be memorialized. Charlesworth described how official tours, publicity materials, an on-site film and specific memorials always refer to the victims as 'people' and 'victims' and never as 'Jews'. In effect this place of memory acted to de-Judaize the concentration camp.

Figure 4.1 *'The present home of Mr and Mrs Jacob Solomon and family, 133 Avenue D, New York City.' Library of Congress, Prints & Photographs Division, FSA-OWI Collection [LC-USF34-T01-009145 DLC]. (Photo by Dorothea Lange)*

Beginning in the 1970s a Polish Catholic sentiment came to the fore at Auschwitz. Cardinal Karol Wojtyla, who was to become Pope John Paul II, held several masses at the camp in which he mentioned a Catholic prisoner of Auschwitz, Father Kolbe, who had favored the conversion of the Jews. Father Kolbe was beatified. At one of these masses an altar featuring a huge cross was constructed at the very location where Jews were unloaded and sent to the gas chambers. Just as before no specific reference to Jews who were killed at the site was

Figure 4.2 *'Out of rear window tenement dwelling of Mr and Mrs Jacob Solomon, 133 Avenue D, New York City.' Library of Congress, Prints & Photographs Division, FSA-OWI Collection [LC-USF34-009114-C DLC]. (Photo by Dorothea Lange)*

made. In 1984 a convent was established at the site of Auschwitz and the contestation of the place of memory became world news as Rabbi Weiss protested the siting of the convent. There is also a church with a huge cross overlooking Auschwitz.

Clearly places have many memories and the question of which memories are promoted and which cease to be memories at all is a

Figure 4.3   *The Statue of Liberty, New York City. Library of Congress, Prints & Photographs Division, Detroit Publishing Company Collection. The Statue of Liberty is a world recognized symbol of the United States which celebrates and memorializes a particular story of American nationhood as a nation of more or less welcome immigrants. It is an official place of memory.*

political question. Places become sites of contestation over which memories to evoke. Kenneth Foote, in his book *Shadowed Ground* (Foote 1997) suggests that places have the power to force hidden and painful memories to the fore through their material existence:

> As a geographer I could not help but notice that the sites themselves seemed to play an active role in their own interpretation. What I mean is that the evidence of violence left behind often pressures people, almost involuntarily, to begin debate over meaning. The sites stained by the blood of violence and covered by the ashes of tragedy, force people to face squarely the meaning of an event. The barbed wire and brick crematoria of the concentration camps cannot be ignored; they demand interpretation. A bare stretch of ground in Berlin, once the Reichssicherheitshauptamt, the headquarters of the Nazi state security, of Gestapo, compels the visitor to reflect on genocide in the twentieth century.   (Foote 1997, 5-6)

The brutal fact of places such as these forces a debate about what they mean and what to do with them. People with differing interests have to make their case for preservation and what is to be included or excluded and thus a new kind of place is born out of a contested process of interpretation. The connection between place and memory

Figure 4.4 *Ellis Island. The Wall of Honor. Ellis Island Immigration Museum memorializes immigration into the United States. Citizens can pay one hundred dollars to have a name of an ancestor engraved on the wall and thus make them a part of 'official memory'. (Photo by Joanne Maddern)*

and the contested nature of this connection has been the object of considerable enquiry by geographers recently and promises to be a major component of geographical research in the future (Johnson 1994, 1996; Till 1999; Hoskins forthcoming; Desforges and Maddern forthcoming).

Gareth Hoskins, for instance, has examined the fate of Angel Island Immigration Station in San Francisco Bay (Hoskins forthcoming). Angel Island was the site of a series of buildings which were used to process Chinese immigrants as they entered the United States. Unlike Ellis Island, on the east coast, this site has not become a site of national memory and celebration of immigrant heritage. Rather it was forgotten and allowed to decay until a few local activists brought it to the attention of politicians and the public. The problem for those who sought to promote it as a place of heritage was that it was a site of deliberate exclusion under the Chinese Exclusion Act of 1882. This was the place where would-be Chinese immigrants were prevented from entering the United States and it does not, therefore, slip easily into a national mythology of inclusion in the 'melting pot'. Hoskins shows how the immigration station was developed by fitting into national

Figures 4.5 and 4.6 *Angel Island and Ellis Island. Unlike Ellis Island, Angel Island, in San Francisco Bay, has not become a nationally celebrated place of memory. While Ellis Island processes mainly European immigrants who have become part of the 'melting pot' ideology of the nation, Angel Island was used to house would-be Chinese immigrants prevented from entering the nation. (Angel Island photo by Gareth Hoskins; Ellis Island photo by Joanne Maddern)*

scale ideologies of belonging and celebration thus obscuring some of the more particular narratives of exclusion and loathing. In order to obtain money and recognition the station had to be reconfigured as part of a general national memory of immigrant belonging that hardly matches its original purpose. As Hoskins puts it:

> part of the price for official approval, national exposure and professional management expertise is that narratives conform more closely to popular and rousing patriotic notions of America where detainees become an object of veneration simply because they personify American ideals. In some cases this diverts attention away from the United States as perpetrator of the racism inscribed in the 1882 Exclusion Act and instead applauds immigrants' ability to overcome oppression at the country of origin by choosing to leave.
> (Hoskins forthcoming)

Here, as in Auschwitz, the politics of memory and politics of place converge.

A nice place to live

'Home' is a concept that reappears throughout this book. As an elementary and ideal (for some) form of place it lies right at the heart of human geography. It is for this reason that the idea of a student making university accommodation into 'their place' was the first example of place in the introduction. Most people are familiar with the attempt to make somewhere feel like home. Even if there are many instances where they do not succeed, the attempt is important. The creation of 'nice places to live' is one of the central ways in which places are produced. But take this activity beyond the seemingly innocent practices of decorating walls and arranging furniture and it soon becomes a political issue.

Let us return, once again, to New York's Lower East Side. As we have seen, by the 1980s the area was subject to gentrification – the purchase of run-down housing at cheap prices by middle class incomers and the subsequent upgrading of the property and massive rise in property values – a process that meant that previous residents of the area could no longer afford to live there.

> Realtors, developers and gentrifiers portrayed as 'urban cowboys' – rugged individualists, driven in pursuit of civic betterment – tame and reclaim the dilapidated communities of the downtown urban frontier. At their hands, city neighbourhoods are transformed as residences are rehabilitated and new luxury apartment complexes are constructed for incoming middle- and

upper-class residents. New boutique landscapes of consumption emerge
catering to their gastronomic, fashion and entertainment demands, and
new landscapes of production are created with the construction of new
office buildings: the workspace of the residents of the 'new' city.

(Reid and Smith 1993, 193)

Laura Reid and Neil Smith argue that this mythology of the frontier (a
boundary where 'savagery' meets 'civilization') hides a process which
is far from benign. Whereas city government and property entre-
preneurs describe the process in the language of improvement
(people returning to the city from the suburbs, historic buildings
being refurbished, nicer restaurants, etc.) there are many people,
poorer people, who are displaced as a new kind of place, a new kind
of 'home' is produced according to middle class tastes and bank
accounts. For a frontier to exist there have to be the two sides of
savagery and civilization. In the Lower East Side the 'working-class,
poor, female-headed households and Latino/Latina and African-
American "natives" of the downtown neighbourhoods' (Reid and
Smith 1993, 195) play the role of the 'savage' in the face of the
'civilization' of expensive loft apartments and cappuccino bars.

Reid and Smith describe the central importance of the arts industry,
city government policy and real estate speculation in the production
of this frontier in the Lower East Side. They describe how the city's
housing policy aimed to promote the gentrification process through
the auctioning off of much of the city-owned housing which had been
available for people who could not afford New York City rents. Part of
the plan was to encourage artists by specifying particular properties
for their use. They sought to play with the area's well-established
reputation as a bohemian and avant-garde kind of place in order to
boost the property prices by attracting in young urban professionals
(Yuppies) who enjoyed the idea of living a little bit dangerously in the
city rather than the suburbs. Alongside this the city government
changed the way it policed and regulated public space in the area. So
called 'undesirables' were removed from parks and other public
places. Prostitutes, drug-dealers, the homeless and kids hanging out
on street corners were cleared from the parks and streets to make the
area a 'nicer place to live' for the incoming gentrifiers. These processes
were all met with resistance from local residents who were opposed to
the gentrification processes. What created a nice 'home' for the
middle-class was experienced as displacement by the poor. Protestors
likened gentrification to 'genocide' and 'class war' rather than the
taming of the frontier. They portrayed gentrification as an attack on
their ways of life, their communities and their 'home'.

Such an alternative scripting of the gentrification process aims at shattering the frontier myths constructed and purveyed by the media, the City and the real estate industry. Gentrification, they argue, is *not* for the good of all and is *not* a progressive development from the perspective of the community and its residents. For them, it means homelessness, displacement, expensive and inaccessible housing, and a challenge to the cultural diversity, practices and tolerance that have been a mark of their neighbourhood.

(Reid and Smith 1993, 199)

Gentrifiers are not the only people with money looking for a 'nice place to live'. A relatively recent development in American town planning is the rise of so-called 'neotraditionalism'. Behind this movement is a desire to create places that are different from the anonymous sprawling suburbs of tract developments and 'MacMansions'. Words such as 'community' and 'history' are often placed at the center of such attempts. The geographer Karen Till has looked at one such place – the urban village of Rancho Santa Margarita in Orange County in California. She argues that the place is created through the invention of traditions to 'validate the establishment of a residential community by providing a sense of historical continuity and stability.' They are, she continues, 'created by corporate planners in order to give the place a sense of identity' (Till 1993, 710)

These planners assert that, unlike their predecessors, they pay attention to the unique nature of places, to their local histories, architectures and urban and residential forms; and to traditional human-land relationships. They maintain that their towns and villages are 'good places to live', places that can 'revive public life', and return the 'bonds of authentic community' to American society.   (Till 1993, 710)

Note how the language that is used by the neotraditionalists reflects the more abstract musings on place by Heidegger, Relph and others – place as an authentic form of dwelling rooted in history. Seemingly abstract and philosophical ideas are rarely confined to the pages of philosophers and theorists.

Till shows how the developers of Rancho Santa Margarita, a totally planned community, attempted to promote the idea of a place rooted in history through materials which focused on the themes of family history and early Californian Spanish colonial architecture. The landowners of the development made a lot of their family history, claiming that they were continuing the traditions of their pioneer forbears. They published so-called 'historical newsletters' with articles about the O'Neills' role in history. The newsletters where made to look old by using tan pages and brown ink. Much was made of the family's generosity in providing land for good causes such as schools and parks.

In addition to the newsletters the promotional material for this new community focused on the 'preservation' of early Californian Spanish colonial architecture which combined red clay tiles roofs, stucco walls and rounded archways.

> The architecture of Rancho Santa Margarita goes back to this early [Californian] tradition. And beyond, when 18th Century Spanish mission-aries built California's first churches, missions and monasteries. Today many of these architectural elements from the past are being preserved in the homes and public buildings of Rancho Santa Margarita.
>
> (Santa Margarita Company quoted by Till 1993, 715)

Till shows how the combination of the family history newsletters and the focus on architecture lock the place into a well-known history of pioneers moving west and settling to produce a distinctive American culture. It is very much the perspective of a white-European land owning elite peopled by rugged cowboys.

> [T]here is little room left for stories from the perspectives of other individuals, including those of women, children, and/or gays from various cultural, ethnic, and socioeconomic backgrounds ... Thus, the promotion of a narrow perspective – one which attempts to silence alternative readings and interpretations of familiar texts and symbols – not only enhances the status of the corporate planners as the community 'experts' who construct 'good places to live', it also imparts social values.   (Till 1993, 717–718)

Here the idea of an authentic place with an authentic past is being manufactured as an image for consumption. It is a form of marketing aimed at getting people to buy houses in Rancho Santa Margarita. The homes themselves, and their so-called 'early Californian Spanish colonial' style is, as Till reports, a selective reproduction of upper-class nineteenth-century romantic visions of earlier missions. The actual buildings are mass-produced by large building companies.

Accompanying this production of a sense of history and authen-ticity is a process of exclusion based on the identification of a threat-ening other beyond the walls of the town. In the case of Rancho Santa Margarita the threatening 'other' is Los Angeles.

> The historic small-town identity that planners would like to foster, however, makes sense only in relation to the place memory of Los Angeles. The success of the former – the small-town identity – depends upon the experience of the latter – present-day suburbs and cities. Both identities

revolve around popular conceptions of current residential experiences in southern California, and both draw upon popularized 'memories' of those experiences in the past, before it became 'bad' and 'dangerous'.

(Till 1993, 722)

As we have seen, throughout this book, the construction of places is more often than not achieved through the exclusion of some 'other' – a constitutive outside. Los Angeles, here, is a place of sin, of social upheaval and moral uncertainty – a dangerous place. It does not take much to see this as a place coding for social others – poor people, the homeless, black people.

In Till's paper then we can see how a 'good place to live' is constructed through the promotion of a particular exclusive history, a selective romanticized architectural vision and a differentiation of Rancho Santa Margarita from a dangerous and disorderly world outside. The example of American neotraditional town planning is not the only example of the attempt to produce a 'good place to live'.

In post-war Britain, politicians and planners were keen to move people out of crowded London and into a ring of 'New Towns' around the metropolis. One of these was and is Crawley. Crawley is not like Rancho Santa Margarita in that it was intended as a place for the 'masses'. New towns have been consistently ridiculed since they were introduced as soulless places full of mass-produced buildings – places that are neither the country nor the city. They are seen as failed places.

The photographer and ex-geography student Sam Appleby decided to explore Crawley armed, as he put it, with a 'camera, memories and French theory' (Appleby 1990, 20). He notes how the new towns were part of an anti-urban ideology that stretches back to the nineteenth century. The idea of the new town was an outgrowth of the earlier 'Garden Cities' such as Letchworth and Welwyn Garden City which had been the result of the ideas of Ebenezor Howard. Howard had seen the miseries of crowded Victorian cities and the backwardness of the rural areas. His idea was to enact a marriage of the city and the country to produce a place with the best of the country and the best of the city combined.

Appleby traces the career of one man, John Goepel, a commissioner for the new town who was responsible for naming the streets of the town for much of its early history. Naming is one of the ways place is given meaning. Tuan has described the role of language in the making of place as a fundamental but neglected aspect of place construction – as important as the material process of building the landscape.

A principle reason for the neglect of speech is that geographers and
landscape historians (and, I believe, people in general) tend to see place
almost exclusively as the result of the material transformation of nature.
They can see farmers chopping down wood and putting up fences and they
can see workers raising the roof beams.   (Tuan 1991a, 684)

Naming, in particular can draw attention to places and locate them in
wider cultural narratives.

To call a feature in the landscape a 'mount' is already to impart to it a
certain character, but to call it 'Mount Misery' is to significantly enhance its
distinctiveness, making it stand out from other rises less imaginatively
called.
...
Naming is power – the creative power to call something into being, to
render the invisible visible, to impart a certain character to things.
                                                          (Tuan 1991a, 688)

Goepel's naming of streets in Crawley reflects this sense of naming as
power. Early on he began giving the streets names he believed
reflected 'Englishness'. These could be historical references such as
'Fleming Way' and 'Newton Road' (named after English scientists) but
more often they referred to elements of a supposed English 'nature'.
Appleby's home area of Langley Green featured streets called 'Hare
Lane', 'Nightingale Close' and 'Juniper Road'. Other streets were
named after figures in English art such as 'Turner Walk' and
'Constable Road'. All of these sought to locate the new town in both
English history and a sense of the countryside – as if they, themselves,
were part of an unproblematic 'nature'. The ideological nature of this
naming process became more apparent when he lost the power to
name and the left-wing town council made Crawley a 'nuclear free
zone' and began to name streets after heroes of the labour and
feminist movements (Pankhurst Court). Goepel believed that 'socialist
mythology' was quite inappropriate for street naming 'evidently only
his own liberal/conservative historicism was capable of providing
natural and fitting themes' (Appleby 1990, 33).

Goepel's naming of streets fits squarely into the anti-urban ideas of
the planning movement's founders. They seek to link the brand new
places into both a sense of history and an identity symbolized by the
English countryside. This mirrors the use of family history and
architectural styles in Rancho Santa Margarita. In both places the
planners are producing their favored sense of place through attempts
to connect the material structure of the two towns into well-known
mythological histories – the story of the frontier in Rancho Santa

Margarita and the nationalist anti-urban mythology in Crawley. Both these stories also seek to create particular place-memories in brand new residential neighborhoods. In this sense these examples are further evidence of the importance of memory and heritage in the production of place.

Regions and nations as places

For the most part geographers' use of place has reflected the common-sense notion of places as being relatively knowable and small scale – cities, towns, neighborhoods. But as Tuan has suggested the idea of place connects the favorite armchair to the globe. So how have geographers considered these larger scale places, the region and the nation? Political geographers have a long tradition of using the concept of place in their research. Notably, they have thought about traditional political divisions in space as having place qualities. The political geographer Peter Taylor notes how writers such as John Agnew and Ron Johnston have utilized place in their work (Taylor 1999). Johnston has written, for instance, about the resistance of Nottinghamshire coal miners to calls for national strikes. He argues that there are specific qualities of Nottinghamshire as a place that made it likely that the miners there would go their own way. Places, in other words, have specific political cultures that trump national and individual arenas (Johnston 1991). Taylor considers the role of space and place in the politics of the modern nation. Nations, he argues, might easily be seen as political impositions of rational and abstract space over the specificities of place. But this argument, he suggests, is too simple and place, too, plays a role in the production of the nation.

> Nations have been constructed as imagined communities each with their own place in the world, their own homeland, some as 'fatherland', others as 'motherland'. By combining state and nation in nation-state, sovereign territory has been merged with sacred homeland to convert a space into a place. (Taylor 1999, 102)

A nation-state is a curious thing. While they seem as natural as the air we breath in the early twenty-first century they are relatively recent creations (for the most part of the nineteenth century). A nation-state, as Taylor suggests, combines the abstraction of space with the deeply-felt emotions of place. How is it that a black inner-city resident of the Bronx feels they belong to the same community as the white business-man in Westchester County and the Mexican immigrant in San

Diego? So much so that, when push comes to shove, many will fight for this thing called the United States. Theorists of the nation suggest that this is because the creation of the nation involves the creation of 'imagined communities' where people with nothing in common in their everyday lives believe themselves to be connected through the idea of a nation as place (Anderson, B. 1991; Edensor 2002). With this place, of course, comes all the paraphernalia of national ideology and belonging – flags, anthems, passports, money and more. For a nation to hold its inhabitants together it must act as place – a field of care.

But within the place of the nation there exist other political units loosely referred to as 'regions'. These places sit, broadly speaking, somewhere between the scale of the nation and the scale of the local. Often the terms region and place are used interchangeably though region does not come with all the philosophical baggage of place (Paasi 2002). Just as politicians have sought to create a national sense of place so local politicians have sought to make politically constituted regions more 'place-like'. While political identity is most often conceived of within the scale of the nation-state: 'sense of place at the national scale can coexist with or be replaced by alternative ones' (Agnew 2002, 6). Politics happens in local and regional places.

In Britain, over the past several decades, there has been a multitude of calls for 'devolution' – the localizing of power into more immediate and small scale 'places'. Wales and Scotland have succeeded in constructing various kinds of regional government. There is ongoing talk of further devolution of powers to areas of England such as Cornwall or the North East. More dramatically, regions of Italy have sought to promote their own political agendas over and above those of the nation-state (Agnew 2002; Giordano 2000). Benito Giordano has provided an account of the claims of Italy's Northern League (Lega Nord), a right wing political party that claims that the Italian state does not serve the people of the North of Italy and is, in effect, in the hands of those in the South. Anti-Southern sentiment is a strong element in their success. As with many forms of place, the place of the 'North' is constructed in relation to its other – the 'South'. Giordano interviews a Northern League councillor:

> The mentality of the people of the North is distinct to that of the South. In the North there is a strong work ethic which could be described as almost Calvinistic in nature. In spite of the high levels of taxation and the burden of the South, Lombardy is still one of the wealthiest regions within the European Union (EU). However, the South of Italy has a 'Mediterranean' work ethic, which is based on corruption, a reliance of state transfers and a more relaxed attitude towards work.   (Quoted in Giordano 2000, 459)

In addition to these crude place stereotypes the Northern League also insist the Italian State is in effect ruled by the South and thus the so-called 'Italian identity' in, in fact a 'Southern Italian' identity. Finally members and supporters of the Northern League identify the South as the source of immigration of people-of-color who they see as a threat to the cultural cohesion of the North. In place of Italy the Northern League advocates the formal constitution of a new region they call 'Padania' consisting of North and Central Italy with its own flag, anthem and forms of government. In order to argue for this new 'space', as Taylor would put it, they have to make it into a 'place' with its own history and customs (of hard work and neo-Calvinism) in order for it to make sense to people. This case confirms the observations of the Finnish geographer, Anssi Paasi that 'regionalization' involves the 'formation of the conceptual or symbolic shape' of what would otherwise be a mere line on a political map. Place symbols such as flags, ceremonies, maps, monuments and all manner of images are constructed to make a place a part of people's lives. Even the naming of a place – Padania – is an important part of making a region into a place (Paasi 1996).

The examples of 'regionalization' in Britain are not quite so politically dramatic but nonetheless important for national and local politics. Sometimes they are applied from national government and are dramatically unsuccessful. Peter Taylor comments on some of the absurdities of regional name designations in Britain.

> How many people in England outside its surrounding area know where Halton (a space with a population of more than 100,000) is? It is in new Cheshire, created by combining old Lancashire's Widnes with Cheshire's Runcorn. Examples such as this could be multiplied many times over but there is another indication of the disrespect for place I wish to note: the proliferation of designated 'boroughs' covering large swathes of rural land. For instance, on travelling north on the Great North Road you enter the 'Borough of Berwick-upon-Tweed' just north of the town of Alnwick, some twenty miles from the town of Berwick itself.   (Taylor 1999, 105)

A similar process has occurred where I live in West Wales where county names have been changed a number of times in recent years between Cardiganshire, Dyfed and Ceredigion in order to construct an appropriate identity for the area. Other regional identities, however, have been fought for from below by people making what they see as deep historical claims to regional identity. Wales and Scotland are obvious examples but areas of England have also made claims for strong regional government based on specific place-identities. The claims from the South West of England ('Wessex' and

Cornwall), for instance, are discussed by Martin Jones and Gordon MacLeod (2001) who show how regional movements mobilize popular local events and mythologies to make claims for the existence of regional identities in political life. Activists in the South West, responding to devolution plans, have called for the creation of region called Wessex (there is no existing county with this name) which they see as 'historically friendly' – a place that people can identify with in distinction to vague simply locational designations such as the 'South West'. The activists argue that while many new 'regions' are simply fabricated (such as those Taylor discusses above) Wessex could make a claim to having an historical existence with its own set of place-images and would therefore be more 'real'.

So the complex entanglement of history and geography that go into making 'place' do not just occur at a cosy local level. The way of knowing that is 'place' is also enacted at the scale of the nation and the region. As we have seen in this section, those who wish to construct relatively large scale political entities cannot simply draw lines on a map and produce them from nothing. They make concerted efforts to give these territories histories and identities in order to make them more place-like and therefore more intelligible to their designated populations.

In Place/Out-of-Place: Anachorism

The creation of place by necessity involves the definition of what lies outside. To put it another way the 'outside' plays a crucial role in the definition of the 'inside.' In many of the examples we have already considered there has been a clear sense of a politics of place production. Rancho Santa Margarita, for instance, has been based on stories that exclude women, black people and Native-Americans (among others). The creation of 'Padania' in Italy by the Northern League has been based on the designation of the Italian South as the 'other'. In the remainder of this chapter we will consider the use of place in research which concerns the politics of place and its role in defining what is appropriate and what is not.

We have repeatedly seen how place is a word that is used often in everyday speech. As such its meaning appears as common-sense and its assumptions are taken-for-granted. Many of these everyday uses link hierarchies in society with spatial location and arrangement. Someone can be 'put in her place' or is supposed to 'know his place.' There is, we are told, 'a place for everything and everything in its place'. Such uses of the term place suggest a tight connection between geographical place and assumptions about normative behavior. People and practices, it seems, can be 'in-place' or 'out-of-place' (Cresswell 1996).

When something or someone has been judged to be 'out-of-place' they have committed a transgression. Transgression simply means 'crossing a line'. Unlike the sociological definition of 'deviance' transgression is an inherently spatial idea. The line that is crossed is often a geographical line and a socio-cultural one. It may or may not be the case that the transgression was intended by the perpetrator. What matters is that the action is seen as transgression by someone who is disturbed by it.

Often, when people, things and practices are seen as 'out-of-place' they are described as pollution and dirt. The anthropologist Mary Douglas defined dirt as 'matter out-of-place.' To be 'out-of-place' depends on pre-existence of a classification system of some kind (Douglas 1966).

> Shoes are not dirty in themselves, but it is dirty to place them on the dining table; food is not dirty in itself, but it is dirty to leave cooking utensils in the bedroom, or food bespattered on clothing, similarly, bathroom equipment in the drawing room; clothes lying on chairs. (Douglas 1966, 36)

The stronger the spatial classification – the greater the desire to expel and exclude – the easier it is to upset those who invest in an existing order. The construction of places, in other words, forms the basis for the possibility of transgression or, in Douglas's terms, pollution. Just as we have a term for thinking about things in the wrong time – anachronism – we might invent a term for things in the wrong place – anachorism.

The use of place to produce order leads to the unintended consequence of place becoming an object and tool of resistance to that order – new types of deviance and transgression such as strikes and sit-ins become possible. The clearer the established meaning and practices of a particular place the easier it is to transgress the expectations that come with place. This is one reason why anti-globalization protestors always pick McDonalds as a target – it is a very clear and well-understood symbol of global capital and the kinds of consumption practices that it encourages.

Recent years have seen an explosion of work which considers the role of place in the production of outsiders – the exclusion of people (and more recently, animals (Philo 1995)) who are said to be 'out-of-place.' Mad people (Parr and Philo 1995; Philo 1987), gypsy-travelers (Sibley 1981), children (Philo 1992; Valentine 1997), political protestors

(Cresswell 1996), non-white people (Craddock 2000; Anderson, K. 1991), gays, lesbians and bisexuals (Bell and Valentine 1995; Brown 2000), the homeless (Veness 1992; Cresswell 2001), prostitutes (Hubbard 1998), the disabled (Kitchin 1998) and a plethora of 'Others' have all been described by the media, local authorities, national governments and others as 'out-of-place' – as not matching the expected relations between place, meanings and practice. Rather then review this whole body of literature I will, instead, focus on the homeless and, first, sexuality 'out-of-place'.

Sexuality out-of-place

The term sexuality refers to the social identities that are built around different forms of sexual desire. Sexualities, in other words, are not just signifiers of different kinds of sexual practice but forms of complicated social and cultural relations. At first glance many people do not see a link between sexuality and place. But like any other form of social relation (class, gender, race, etc.) it is constituted, in part, geographically. It is fairly common-place for instance, to hear people suggest that gay sexuality is fine just so long as it does not occur in public places. To back up this argument it might be claimed that heterosexuality belongs 'at home' or 'in the bedroom' so homo-sexuality does too.

Much of the work on sexuality in geography has sought to show how such claims are absurd. Heterosexuality occurs everywhere (Duncan 1996). Straight people feel free to kiss in public or walk down the street hand in hand. Public spaces such as law courts and govern-ment offices formally institutionalize hetero-relations while making gay relationships illegal. Everywhere we look straight sexuality is accepted as normal and is thus invisible to straight people. Gay people, on the other hand, see heterosexuality everywhere and through this experience their own sexuality as radically 'out-of-place'. All it takes is for a gay couple to kiss in a public place for hetero-outrage to come to the fore. The geographer Michael Brown has studied the spatiality of gay sexuality at length. His book *Closet Space* examines the ways in which gay sexuality is maginalized and made invisible at all scales (Brown 2000). He describes a scene on a bus in which these tensions and expectations are made dramatically clear.

> The Seattle Metro bus no. 7 stopped abruptly to pick up two very wet people just at the crest of Capital Hill on a rainy Tuesday afternoon. The sudden braking caught everyone's attention, and broke the passionate soul

kissing of a man and woman sitting just across from me. Since I was sitting towards the rear of the dingy bus, I had a long view of a slender, trendy woman making her way purposefully down the aisle. Behind her, I heard her companion before I could see him. We all could, because he was speaking so loudly. With a mixture of aplomb and hubris our new rider proclaimed, 'That's right, people, I'm swinging my hips as I walk on by. And if you don't like it, you can kiss my beautiful queer ass!' With regal camp he sashayed down the aisle, past my seat, never once breaking his stare forward. On the other side of the aisle, the young heterosexual couple 'tsked', huffed and 'Oh, Gawwwwd'-ed this young gay man audibly enough to make their revulsion clear to those of us in the back of the bus. 'Who said that?' the gay man demanded loudly.

Everyone on the bus began to grow visibly uncomfortable. After all, this was Seattle. 'I did,' the woman stated loud and clear, but without turning to face him. Then she whispered something inaudible to her boyfriend and they both laughed. 'Well if you don't like it, girlfriend, *what the hell you doin'* up on Capitol Hill in the first place!'   (Brown 2000, 27)

As Brown observes there is a complicated set of interactions between the performance of sexuality and expectations about place in this event. To the heterosexual couple all space is straight space. Places such as the city and the bus sustained heteronormativity – the idea that heterosexuality is normal, natural and appropriate. They felt that they could kiss passionately in public. The gay man, to them, was acting out-of-place – disturbing the unspoken rules of sexuality. To the gay man, however, this was Capitol Hill, a gay area in Seattle. To him the straight couple were 'out-of-place' and should consider keeping their sexuality, and certainly their homophobia – 'in the closet'. The idea of the closet is a complicated one which acts at all scales 'from the body to the globe' (the subtitle of Brown's book). This metaphorical closet is a certain kind of place that is both a place of secrecy and a place of autonomy and safety. The closet is a place where a person can keep their sexuality entirely to themselves or it can, more literally, become a building or an area of the city where it is safe to be gay. It can also be a confining prison.

This issue of the closet and heteronormative space has become central to the geographical analysis of sexuality. Geographers have asked why some places seem to be safe places for certain sexualities to be performed while other places pressure gays, lesbians and bisexuals to keep their sexualities to themselves. The work of Gill Valentine has been central to this line of thinking. She has shown how lesbians have had to consistently conceal their sexuality in certain kinds of places – particularly home and work – in order to avoid discrimination and hatred. The women she has interviewed reveal incredibly complicated

daily lives of concealment in some places and being 'out' in others.
Some of them had to travel miles to feel comfortable away from both
family (parents and siblings) and workmates (Valentine 1993).

There are many different identities gay, lesbian and bisexual people
can choose to perform, just as there are many identities straight
people can perform (hell's angel, 'new man', power-dresser, etc.).
David Bell, John Binnie, Julia Cream and Gill Valentine explore two of
these identities the 'gay skinhead' and the 'lipstick lesbian' in their
paper 'All hyped up and no place to go'.

> Through the deployment of the 'gay skinhead' and 'lipstick lesbian' and the
> places they produce and occupy, we hope to illuminate the 'unnaturalness'
> of both heterosexual everyday space and masculine and feminine
> heterosexual identities associated with them. The exposure of the
> fabrication of both seamless heterosexual identities and the straight spaces
> they occupy should shatter the illusion of their just *being*, of simply
> naturally occurring.   (Bell *et al.* 1994, 32 emphasis in original)

A 'lipstick lesbian' is a lesbian who dresses in a hyper-feminine way
thus challenging the popular conception of lesbian women as
masculine figures. The figure of the lipstick lesbian, to some people,
mocks heterosexual expressions of femininity in a way that is more
subtle than the butch drag of other lesbians. Their appearance, it is
claimed, 'undermines a heterosexual's ability to determine whether
feminine women in everyday spaces are lesbian or heterosexual' (Bell
et al. 1994, 42). This uncertainty, created by images of femininity in
heterosexual places, means that straight people can no longer assume
the accepted codes of everyday life and thus heterosexual places are
undermined. In a twist to the tale, though, the authors acknowledge
that this subversion depends on straight people being aware of the
existence of lipstick lesbians in the first place. Since most straight
people assume the normal and natural condition of heteronormativity
it seems likely that most of them are unaware of the subversions going
on around them. To wake them out of their slumber they are more
likely to be provoked by the gay man on Brown's bus in Seattle.

A transgressive act that was definitely noticed was the Greenham
Common Women's Peace Camp in the early 1980s. Women camped
outside the US Air Force base from 1981 onwards to protest the cruise
missiles that were being based there. In their view the cruise missiles,
armed with nuclear warheads, were 'out-of-place' in the United
Kingdom. Soon local residents of nearby Newbury, Berkshire began
to object to the peace camp. Government figures and the media, for a
period of several years, used every metaphor they could think of to

describe the women as 'out-of-place'. These included obligatory references to dirt, disease, madness and, of-course, sexuality (Cresswell
1994).

The *Sun* (19 November 1983) claimed that the women 'are not
people – they're all burly lesbians'. News reports frequently suggested
that the fact that this was an all women's camp automatically meant
that the vast majority of the protesters were lesbians. The fact that
they dressed in 'masculine' clothes and were frequently dirty only
seemed to confirm this impression. The *Daily Mail* (13 January 1983)
paints a picture of multiple transgression:

> And there's Eve breastfeeding by the fire, a vague, amiable, ever smiling
> lesbian mother from Islington who's camping here with her two children,
> aged eight and six months by different fathers, one of them West Indian.
>
> (quoted in Cresswell 1994, 49)

Eve is clearly a figure 'out-of-place' here. She is breastfeeding in a
public place, she is a lesbian and she has children with multiple
fathers including one (we must assume) who is black.

> [H]alf the women I lived among at Greenham were lesbians, striding the
> camp with their butch haircuts, boots and boilersuits. They flaunt their
> sexuality, boast about it, joke about it. And some take delight in proclaiming
> their loathing of men ... I was shocked on my first day when two peace
> women suddenly went into passionate embrace in full view of everyone ...
> And gradually I became annoyed at the way doting couples sat around the
> camp fire kissing and caressing ... A lot of women 'go gay' after arriving at
> the camp. With no men around they have to turn to each other for comfort.
>
> (quoted in Cresswell 1994, 50)

Here, the *Daily Express's* undercover investigator, Sarah Bond, acts in
the same way as the woman on the bus described by Brown. She sees
women kissing in a place she considers inappropriate and is disgusted
– she described it as flaunting. Do straight people 'flaunt' their
sexuality when they kiss in a public place? Bond is arguing that this
kind of activity should be put back in to the closet – should be replaced. To Bond, lesbian sexuality is 'out-of-place' at Greenham
Common. The reference to the absence of men at the end of the
extract implies that women only turn to each other in places without
men. Behind this lies the missing place of 'home' where husbands
would undoubtedly be available for 'comfort'.

The understanding of sexualities-out-of-place should not be restricted to supposedly marginal sexualities. Ignoring heterosexualities
only serves to reinforce the notion that heterosexuality is normal and

thus invisible (Hubbard 2000). For the most part heterosexual activity and the wider sense of identity that surrounds it remains the norm by which other forms of sexuality are implicitly and explicitly judged. The idea of 'home' for instance – the ideal place – is quite clearly heteronormative. Recent research has shown how the idea of home and actual homes themselves are constructed as places for traditional families. Homeliness does not properly arrive until the children arrive (Valentine 1993). It is this heterosexual home that lies behind many of the descriptions of the Greenham Women as 'out-of-place'.

Some of the most interesting work on sexuality and place has been on heterosexual prostitution. Research has shown how prostitution is seen as 'out-of-place' in some places while it is almost acceptable in others (Hubbard 1998). Philip Hubbard has outlined a number of arguments about the 'place' of prostitution in England. He notes that there is a generally recognized distinction between 'high class' prostitutes who work in 'private' spaces and 'lower class' prostitutes who work on the street and in public space. While the former is usually ignored due to the assumption that sexuality gets expressed in private spaces (an illusion shown to be false by queer theorists in particular) the latter has been the object of considerable moral panics in British cities such as Birmingham and Bradford where local residents' groups have enacted pickets of prostitutes in order to kerb what they see as a public nuisance.

The law in Britain seeks to make prostitution in public places less visible but, as Hubbard argues, 'dominant moral geographies appear to dictate this visibility is more acceptable in some spaces than others' (Hubbard 1997, 133). These spaces where prostitution is deemed to be 'in-place' are commonly known as red-light districts. These places are typically in economically marginal spaces of the city and can, in Hubbard's terms be seen as 'a part of a continuing (but contested) process involving the exclusion of disorderly prostitution from orderly sexuality (or "bad girls" from "good girls"), removing prostitutes from areas where they would stand out as unnatural or deviant, potentially "polluting" civilised society' (Hubbard 1997, 135). Hubbard reveals how policing strategies often overlook prostitution in designated areas or 'toleration zones' in order that they might better exclude prostitutes from elsewhere. Thus places of abjection are created and tolerated on the margins of city centers.

In work on the geography of sexuality the word 'place' is often used interchangeably with the word 'space'. It is important to bear in mind, therefore, the specific analytical qualities of place that make it important in these studies. The idea of being 'out-of-place' or 'in-place' is admittedly a simple one, but one that nonetheless conveys a sense of the way segments of the geographical world are meaningful and how those meanings both produce and are reproduced by people and their practices. A saying from Sri Lanka states; 'The fish don't talk about the water'. What this means is that we rarely explicitly become aware of and talk about that which we take for granted. To a fish the water is their taken-for-granted world. People have environments too – environments made up of meaningful places. What the geographers of sexuality have shown us is that these places more often than not contribute to the invisible and unstated normalization and naturalization of particular kinds of sexuality. Other kinds of sexuality – gay, lesbian, bisexual, commercial – threaten the links between space, meaning and practice that make up 'place' and suggest other ways of being – other possible meanings – new kinds of place.

The homeless – people without place

The idea of 'home' as an ideal kind of place has particularly negative consequences for the homeless – people without place. In his 1991 paper 'A View of Geography' Yi-Fu Tuan described geography as the study of Earth as the home of people (Tuan 1991b). The central concept for Tuan is 'home'.

> Home obviously means more than a natural of physical setting. Especially, the term cannot be limited to a built place. A useful point of departure for understanding home may be not its material manifestation but rather a concept: home is a unit of space organized mentally and materially to satisfy a people's real and perceived basic biosocial needs and, beyond that, their higher aesthetic-political aspirations. (Tuan 1991b, 102)

In other words home, for Tuan, is a kind of ideal place. 'Home, insofar as it is an intimately lived in place, is imbued with moral meaning' (Tuan 1991b, 105). These reflections on place as home are, of course, open to critique at the theoretical level. We have already seen how feminists, for instance, have argued that home is often far from the cosy moral universe Tuan suggests (Rose 1993; Martin and Mohanty 1986). Indeed home can be an oppressive, confining and even terrifying place for many people – especially for abused women and children. Earlier in this chapter we say how the idealized view of home is one based around a heterosexual family. But the perception of place as home also has consequences for those without readily apparent places to call home.

Anthropologist, Liisa Malkki has argued that there is a tendency in the modern world to locate people and identities in particular spaces and within particular boundaries (Malkki 1992). He belongs there, she belongs here. One result of this is to think of people without place in wholly negative ways. Connected to this, she goes on, are ways of thinking which are also rooted and bounded. She suggests that it is our incessant desire to divide the world up into clearly bounded territorial units which produces a 'sedentarist metaphysics.' Fixed, bounded and rooted conceptions of culture and identity, she argues, are linked to particular ways of thinking which are themselves sedentary. These ways of thinking then reaffirm and enable the common-sense segmentation of the world into things like nations, states, counties and places. Thinking of the world as rooted and bounded is reflected in language and social practice. Such thoughts actively territorialize identities in property, in region, in nation – in place and they simultaneously produce thoughts and practices that treat mobility and displacement as pathological. Malkki provides the example of a post-war report of refugees:

> Homelessness is a serious threat to moral behaviour ... At the moment the refugee crosses the frontiers of his own world, his whole moral outlook, his attitude toward the divine order of things, changes ... [The refugees'] conduct makes it obvious that we are dealing with individuals who are basically amoral, without any sense of personal or social responsibility ... They no longer feel themselves bound by ethical precepts which every honest citizen ...respects. They become a menace, dangerous characters who will stop at nothing.   (quoted in Malkki 1992, 32)

Here we see a clear connection made between people moving out of the place they 'belong' and perceived amorality and danger. In this sense place is much more than a thing in the world – it also frames our ways of seeing and understanding the world. In philosophical terms place is more than a question of ontology (what exists) but, perhaps more fundamentally) a question of epistemology (how we know things). One way in which place as a concept can be used empirically and theoretically, then, is to look at 'people without place'. Consider the homeless, and refugees.

Home and homelessness

Homelessness has, as far as we know, always been present in human society in one form or another. To be homeless does not simply mean to be without what we (inhabitants of the contemporary developed world for the most part) would call a home. Homelessness is very much defined by a certain kind of disconnection from particular forms of place. Historians and theorists often point of the English vagrancy scares of Elizabethan times as an important historical point in the formation of ideas about homelessness. It was at this time that a large number of people, formally tied to the land of their masters, were freed from feudal ties and started to wander the land. They were known as 'masterless men' which meant both that they served no lord and that they were 'without place.' Here place means both a geographical location and a clear place in a social hierarchy that was beginning to dissolve. The sociologist Zygmunt Bauman described these vagabonds as 'the advanced troops or guerilla units of post-traditional chaos ... and they had to go if order ... was to be the rule. The free-roaming vagabonds made the search for new, state-managed, societal-level order imperative and urgent' (Bauman 1995, 94).

One element of this transformation – from feudalism to early-capitalism – was the displacement of thousands of people from the land and the villages they had formerly belonged to. These 'vagrants' and 'masterless men' created a new measure of uncertainty about the traditional patterns of rights and duties. In short they were seen as people without place and were thus a threat to the most fundamental forms of order.

> What made the vagabond so terrifying was his apparent freedom to move and so to escape the net of the previously locally based control. Worse than that, the movements of the vagabond were unpredictable; unlike the pilgrim or, for that matter, a nomad, the vagabond has no set destination. You do not know where he will move next, because he himself does not know or care much.   (Bauman 1995, 94)

The mobility of the vagabond is key for Bauman. Unlike other mobile people such as tourists and nomads the vagabonds' mobility was totally unpredictable and thus threatening. The vagabond's wayward travels meant that he always had traces of elsewhere about him which disturbed those who had chosen a settled and rooted existence – the vagabond threatened to undo the comforts of place and transgressed the expectations of a sedentarist metaphysics.

While we rarely talk of vagrancy in the twenty-first century, homelessness is still very much a contentious issue throughout the world. What has not changed is the fact that homelessness cannot be understood adequately without recourse to an examination of the kinds of places that produce it. While Elizabethan vagrancy needs to be seen in the light of feudal understandings of the place of the poor, contemporary homelessness need to be seen in relation to the kinds of places that are being produced in the contemporary city and countryside.

Neil Smith has researched and written about the homeless in Tompkins Square Park in New York's Lower East Side during the 1980s and 1990s (Smith 1996). It was at this time that Mayor Dinkins tried to remove the homeless from the park. We saw earlier in this chapter how the control of public space was one aspect of the wider processes of gentrification. The Lower East Side had been an area of the city ignored by the city government and by business. Low property prices had attracted middle class gentrifiers back into the area (see above). The new 'yuppie' residents had a particular vision of the kind of place they wanted to live in and it did not include home-less people in 'their' park. The homeless were perceived and represented as a threat to both their personal safety and, perhaps more importantly, their property values. It was in this context that Dinkins attempted to remove the homeless people who spent the night in the park. He used the dictionary definition of 'park' to make his point:

> A park is not a shantytown. It is not a campground, a homeless shelter, a shooting gallery for drug addicts or political problem. Unless it is Tompkins Square Park in Manhattan's East Village.
>   (Mayor Dinkins quoted in Smith 1996, 220)

Here Dinkins is making a direct claim about the kind of place a park is. This kind of place, he is arguing, is not the kind of place you sleep in. For this reason the park needed to be reclaimed from the homeless.

This line of argumentation is remarkably similar to that of his predecessor Mayor Koch who had also been annoyed by the sight of the homeless in his city (Koch had actually begun the process of removing the homeless from Tompkins Square calling the park a 'cesspool'). Reacting to the presence of the homeless in Grand Central Station he had attempted to introduce an anti-loitering law giving the police the powers to remove the homeless from public spaces. The State Supreme Court had overturned the law and Koch had responded in a speech to the American Institute of Architects. In the question and answer session at the end of the speech Koch reminded the architects of the homeless people in Grand Central Station.

> These homeless people, you can tell who they are. They're sitting on the floor, occasionally defecating, urinating, talking to themselves ... We thought it would be reasonable for the authorities to say, 'you can't stay here unless you're here for transportation.' Reasonable, rational people would come to the same conclusion, right? Not the Court of Appeals.
>   (Mayor Koch quoted in Deutsche 1988, 5)

Both Koch and Dinkins are making arguments about the meaning of place in their tirades against the homeless. Koch claims that 'reasonable people' would agree that a railroad station is a place for traveling. Dinkins uses the authority of Webster's Dictionary to point out that the definition of park does not include a place to sleep. Both of them, by making these appeals to 'common-sense', take the issue of homelessness out of its wider context in the economic and political geography of New York City. The right wing critic George Will went even further when he wrote in 1988 that:

> It is illegal to litter the streets, frankly it ought to be illegal ... to sleep in the streets. Therefore, there is a simple matter of public order and hygiene in getting these people somewhere else. Not arrest them, but move them off somewhere where they are simply out of sight.
>
> (George Will quoted in Smith 1996, 28)

Homelessness is treated simply as instances of 'people out-of-place' – as a human form of litter – rather than as a symptom of the urban politics and economics of New York. As Neil Smith, Rosalyn Deutsche and others have argued – to answer questions about homelessness we need to look at the city as a social space in which homelessness occurs – spaces of the city reveal the conditions that produce homelessness. Homelessness is produced through the push to reconstruct the city as a cohesive place according to middle class/elite values.

But it is not only the city where the homeless are seen as 'out-of-place'. Paul Cloke, Paul Milbourne and Rebekah Widdowfield have collaborated on a project to examine the connection that is usually made between urban places and homelessness – a connection that, in their view, makes rural homelessness all but invisible (Cloke et al. 2000). Very few academic considerations of homelessness have focused on rural homelessness. Homelessness, it seems, has its place – and that place is the city. The countryside – the rural – has most often been seen as a place away from the problems of urbanity. It is for this reason that the street names of Crawley were so bucolic. The countryside is portrayed as a problem-free realm of peace and tranquillity. This image of the rural, known as the 'rural idyll', has deep roots in British history with the romantic vision of a 'green and pleasant land.' This image has, of course, changed over recent years with issues such as Mad Cow Disease, Foot and Mouth and the increasing visibility of rural poverty. Nevertheless rural homelessness has hardly been a headline issue. As Cloke et al. remark there are morphological and sociocultural reasons for the 'noncoupling of homelessness and rurality' (Cloke et al. 2000, 718). Morphologically rural places simply do not provide the kinds of spaces where homeless people might gather and become visible. In addition some of the rural homeless choose to spend their nights under hedges and in the woods where they will not be seen and harassed. Socio-culturally rural residents often deny that problems exist in the areas they inhabit. Here the pervasive myth of the rural idyll seems to be strong still. An interview with Louie, a Parish Councillor from Devon illustrates this problem:

Interviewer: Do you know of any problems of homelessness in the village?

Louie: There isn't any homelessness here. We have a good, helpful community. If folks are in trouble we help them. All the undesirables keep themselves to themselves or move away. We've had some lovely people come to live here.

Interviewer: What would you do if you saw a homeless person in the village?

Louie: Well I'd die of shock, I think. We just don't get that round here – in Exeter maybe, but not out here.

As the authors point out Louie can only contemplate homelessness by displacing it to the urban environment of Exeter. The countryside has been constituted by both its inhabitants and by policymakers and government officials as a 'pure space'. Cloke *et al.* draw on the work of David Sibley to make this point:

the countryside, it seems, belongs to the middle class, to landowners and to people who engage in blood sports. A rigid stereotype of place, the English countryside, throws up discrepant others. These groups are other, they are folk-devils, and they transgress only because the countryside is defined as a stereotypical pure space which cannot accommodate difference.

(Sibley quoted in Cloke *et al.* 2000, 727)

Another aspect of rural place that Cloke *et al.* draw our attention to is the tight connection between the very idea of 'home' and rurality. Part of the rural idyll is a particular idea of domesticity and family. This is as true of the Cotswolds as it is of rural Iowa with the well-known imagery of 'mom and apple pie'. 'Being without a home, then, in geographic space where the *imagined* geography is one where the home is valorized to this extent, is once again to transgress the sociocultural meanings and moralities which lie at the heart of rural life' (Cloke *et al.* 2000, 730).

This connection between home and rurality was also evident in reactions to the tramp in the United States in the latter part of the nineteenth century and the first three decades of the twentieth century. Following the economic collapse of 1873 and the completion of the first transcontinental railroad in 1869 many people were made homeless. For the first time they were mobile on a continental scale – able to move from coast to coast within a week or two. These people were called tramps. One reaction to them was to label them a threat to women in rural homes. Stories circulated about tramps coming to doors at night, when the man of the house was away, and threatening women and the domesticity they embodied. The *Philadelphia Press* of 14 July 1907 reported that 'the newspapers have each day printed one instance, often two, of women walking ... in the rural districts of Eastern Pennsylvania or Southern New Jersey, who have fled it terror from some tramp or vagrant' (quoted in Cresswell 2001, 93). The biggest threat though was thought to be the moment when the tramp visited the home. Henry Rood in the *Forum* in 1889 observed that there are 'few mothers and fewer daughters who, under such circumstances, would refuse to give food or clothing to a burly, unkempt tramp, who accompanied his request with threatening expression' (quoted in Cresswell 2001, 94). This moment of threat was also the subject of cartoons and posters. An illustration in *Harpers* magazine in 1876 shows a pathetic but threatening tramp asking for money or food while a motherly figure retreats with wooden spoon in hand. The table is laid and dinner is cooking. Outside other men wander. The home, a place at the heart of American national mythology, was clearly under threat from the homeless.

In a more profound way homelessness is very much a product of the idea of 'home' as a particular kind of place. In the western world 'Home' is an ideal as well as a place – a spatially constructed ideology usually correlated with housing. At its most basic level homelessness denotes a lack of housing. But homelessness also signifies 'displacement' – an existential lack that is perhaps even more fundamental than being without shelter. Jon May explores this notion of 'home as place' through an exploration of the life-histories of people living in various forms of shelter for the homeless (May 2000). His interviews with these men often evoke a sense of loss-of-place far deeper than simply the loss of a home is a restricted sense. Take his interview with Michael for instance:

Interviewer: Why leave London?'
Michael: I dunno. I just wanted some place new. Get out of it. I was fed up with it [long pause]. You know, erm, I probably didn't think about it to be honest ... I wasn't going to stay where I was [in a hostel following the separation from his wife] so I said, well, 'anywhere has got to be better than this'.

Interviewer:	So moving wasn't like a wrench for you?
Michael:	No, I wouldn't say that [it wasn't as if] I was leaving anything behind, you know? I mean you've just got to pack your bags and you're off.
Interviewer:	And does this feel like your town now?
Michael:	[Ironic laughter] I don't know [pause]. Yeah, I suppose it is – at the moment ... But at the end of the day you always talk about 'going home' don't you? ... I mean, I've made friends with a few people [pause] you know, go for a drink and that. Fine, but ... no, I wouldn't call this place my home ... where you come from's home isn't it?
	(Interview with Michael, age 33, 4 December 1997 in May 2000, 748)

As May argues, the notion of displacement suggests a previous experience of home as place 'one reaching beyond the boundaries of residence to include that wider sense of belonging more usually described as a "sense of place"' (May 2000, 748).

But as April Veness has shown, homelessness is also a term of disrespect for those who do not fit into a conception of home – who do not fit prevailing standards of housing, land tenure, family form and material comfort (Veness 1992). Through both historical research and ethnographic work with homeless people Vaness shows how what counts as 'home' has historically shrunk and boundaries have

Figure 4.7 *Illustration from* Harper's magazine *(1876). Here the domestic space of the home, complete with woman, child and dinner on the table, is threatened by the tramp who comes to the door.*

become more rigid. Forms of housing such as council housing, mobile homes, shelters, bedsits and student lodging have become increasingly suspect, particularly since World War II. All of these appear to be less-than-home within an ideology that equates the notion of home with private home ownership. Even then it is preferable that the home is a detached one. This ideology of home can be seen in Margaret Thatcher's 'right to buy' scheme in the 1980s where council house owners were told that they would not really have a proper home unless they owned it. Home is very much a category that defines normality.

As 'home' became increasingly restrictive in the kind of shelter that it applied to so more and more people became 'homeless.' Simultaneously the homeless appeared to be more and more transgressive as their lives were out of compliance with the rosy ideology of the property pages. Some of the homeless people Veness and May talk to think of themselves as having places to call home – even when they were sleeping rough – but these places simply do not count in the eyes of those who encounter them. The close connection between place, identity and morality creates a world that is difficult for some of those who are apparently 'without place'.

Refugees

Refugees and asylum-seekers are at the center of the moral panic of the age. Seemingly daily we hear about asylum seekers entering the UK through the Channel Tunnel, Afghans trying to get into Australia, Albanians into Italy or Mexicans into the United States. Rarely, on the other hand, do we (here in the Western world) hear about the refugees in Pakistan (for instance) where the numbers involved are much larger. Reporting on refugees in recent times points towards the comparative over-abundance of reporting on refugees as a 'crisis'. In many cases the argument is made for measures to crack down on the refugees and asylum seekers so that it is not so 'easy' for them to enter Britain, Italy or Australia. At first glace we might suppose that the idea of 'place' is not particularly relevant to understanding this issue. But, as with the homeless, ideas about place are right at the heart of the definition of refugees as a 'problem' – as people 'out-of-place'.

Despite the seemingly contemporary nature of the refugee 'problem' it is necessary to see the refugee as an historical figure. The following is a précis of the history given by Saskia Sassen in her book *Guests and Aliens* (Sassen 1999). Refugee is a term specifically designed to refer to Protestants who were forced to leave France at the end of the seventeenth century. By the eighteenth century the term was being more widely used to describe anyone leaving his or her country in times of distress. By the nineteenth century it was usually used to refer to well-educated elites who had left their homeland such as Polish aristocrats in France. It was towards the end of the nineteenth century that large numbers of relatively poor refugees became a feature of European life. The Franco-Prussian wars alone (1864–1871) created huge number of displaced people with twelve million men fighting against France.

As nation-states became a feature of European life anxieties grew about being ruled by 'foreigners'. When the Germans took over Alsace-Lorraine, France expelled 80,000 Germans and 130,000 French people left for France. Often these were poor refugees – working class and often politically radical. Even so, many places welcomed them as extra labor. At the same time the industrial revolution and the end of serfdom in Austria (1848) and Russia (1861) were transforming European geographies of movement. Masses of people were newly mobile. The construction of railroads in Europe, for instance, made use of migrant workers from Ireland, Italy and elsewhere. Outside of Europe colonialism meant mass migration overseas. Between 1840 and 1900, 26 million people left Europe. For many, the new mass geographical mobility did not correspond to social mobility.

> In this the condition of the new migrants approached, again, that of the political refugees. The struggle for survival consumed their energies rather than a coherent narrative of ambition. For the new masses of migrants and refugees, the geography of movement became a vector of change without a secure destination. They revolved on fortune's wheel, rather than pursued a fate.   (Sassen 1999, 45)

By World War I over two million Jews had left Eastern Europe and many more refugees had been created by the Ottoman Empire. The concept of 'foreigner' or 'outsider' began to connote allegiance to states.

World War II signaled the emergence of the modern refugee crisis. State sovereignty became a central form of power and borders were increasingly policed. Passports were more or less invented around this time. An inward looking United States made it harder and harder for refugees and migrants to enter the country and this forced Europeans to deal with refugees coming from the East. Refugees were increasingly seen as people who did not belong to the host national society and therefore were not entitled to rights of citizenship. Citizenship was tied to place. As with vagabonds and transients before them this 'being without place' was a source of anxiety. The state reacted to this anxiety by identifying them and regulating them.

What this pocket history shows us is that the refugee is a profoundly European product – founded on the organization of the nation-state at the turn of the century in Europe. The drawing and policing of national borders, the firming up of state sovereignty and the construction of national identities were all necessary conditions for the production of the refugee as a person 'out-of-place'. The place they were out of was the nation and that was itself a relatively recent phenomenon.

The modern refugee is legally defined by Article 1 of the Geneva Convention Relating to the Status of Refugees, 1951 and the 1967 New York Protocol to the Convention Relating to the Status of Refugees. The relevant passage reads as follows:

> Owing to a well-founded fear of being persecuted for reasons of race, religion, nationality, membership of a social group or political opinion, is *outside the country of his nationality* and is unable, or owing to such fear is unwilling to avail himself of the protection of that country; or who, not having a nationality and being outside the country of his former habitual residence as a result of such events is unable, or, owing to such fear, is unwilling to return to it.　　　　(Geneva Convention in Tuitt 1996, 12)

Central to this legal definition is the concept of alienage (being from elsewhere) and transborder mobility. You cannot be an internal refugee. As Tuitt has argued law uses the transborder mobility of the refugee to construct a limited definition and therefore limited obligations for host nations.

> Transborder movement – as an identifying feature of the phenomenon of refugeehood – is clearly at odds with images of the very young who lack the basic sustenance to move beyond that required for elementary functions. The concept of alienage, at its most basic level of understanding, is separate from the reality that drought, famine and similar causes of human suffering, by their nature immobilise large sections of the population, particularly the young and vulnerable and those upon whom they depend　　　　　　　　　　　　　　　(Tuitt 1996, 12–13)

By limiting the definition of refugee to those who are able to move the perception of refugees in the host country focused on a population determined by their ability to move – a population that is overwhelmingly adult and male.

The movement of refugees from one state to another poses a question of the moral and legal use of sovereign power of states to admit aliens into their territory. As people-without-place refugees represent a crisis point in state power. The appearance of refugees and asylum seekers in the United Kingdom, for instance has been met with repressive and reactionary calls to protect 'our place' against the alleged 'flood' of incomers who, it is said do not 'belong' here. One reaction – the 1996 Asylum and Immigration Act sought to counter the non place specific intent of the Geneva Convention by producing a White List of countries that were deemed to be safe. Anyone claiming asylum from these places could then be automatically refused based purely on the place they originated.

Reactions to refugees and asylum seekers in the right wing press and by government officials from both major political parties are full of metaphors of fluidity. Allen White has commented on the story circulating in 2001 that asylum seekers and illegal immigrants had introduced the foot and mouth virus into the United Kingdom's herd of cattle. It is a story, he argues, that matches the intense pathologization of refugees, asylum seekers and immigrant in general.

> In the UK, hydraulic metaphors imagine flows of migrants (water, blood, diseases) leaving and entering states (reservoirs, lake or the body) that are protected by international borders and immigration laws (dams or surgical instruments). Flows may be 'out-of-control' threatening the livelihoods of all citizens, thus 'floods' of refugees or asylum seekers threaten to 'swamp' the state. Representing the state and refugee movements in such a simplistic, but seductively holisitic, way legitimates the replacement of polyvocal, complex and chaotic stories and realities of migrant life with a monochrome universe of truth.   (White 2002, 1055)

These metaphors of fluidity have a long and controversial history in the United Kingdom. Peter Jackson traces some of the history of these metaphors noting how they were used by the government minister, Enoch Powell in speeches about immigration in the 1960s, Margaret Thatcher in her 1979 election bid and in the press at the time of the introduction of compulsory visas for visitors to Britain from some parts of the non-white Commonwealth in 1986. The *Sun* headline read '3,000 Asians flood Britain' while the *Daily Express* read 'Asian flood swamps airport' (Jackson 1989, 143–144). Despite the outrage expressed each time these metaphors have been used they have become even more prevalent in the 1990s and beyond as the moral panic about refugees and asylum seekers has risen to new heights. The *Daily Telegraph* of 27 October 1995, for instance, read 'Asylum Seekers: Dutch stem the flood of illegal immigrants' (*Daily Telegraph* 27 October 1995). Government ministers frequently talk of the 'rising tide' of asylum applications and speak of 'flood gates' being blown asunder. These metaphors are 'out-of-place' metaphors. They insinuate that place, boundaries (floodgates) and stability are under siege from the fluid and mobile refugees. Not only are the refugees and asylum seekers from other places but they supposedly threaten 'our place' and 'our culture'.

The image of the refugee and asylum seeker in Britain has been heavily racialized. Refugees are conflated with different races in the argument that accepting more in the country will threaten internal race relations. In these arguments the focus is invariably on non-white refugees. The focus on the racial/ethnic origins of refugees diverts attention from the reasons for migration and promotes the view that refugee control is in fact control of 'economic migrants.' It is easier to make a case against people labeled economic migrants than refugees. Refugees are also criminalized. They are accused of wholesale fraudulent transactions with social security and more recently a direct connection has been drawn between refugees and terrorists. This has led to compulsory fingerprinting of all applicants for asylum regardless of evidence, the holding of asylum seekers in detention centers and discriminatory housing law. As long as people without place are treated as criminals they will probably be seen as criminals.

So called 'new asylum seekers' – mostly non-white people who are engaged in inter-continental travel are a post 1970 phenomenon. These new asylum seekers (new, that is, to the Western world) challenged the previous 'white' image of refugees fostered by the convention which was drawn up with reference to white Europeans. It is these people – non-white asylum seekers who are often described as 'bogus' or 'economic migrants'. Language such as this continues the process of constructing the refugee as a problem and as a threat to 'our place'. In addition, once they get here, they are said to take away resources which rightly belong to 'our' people:

> What gives *the asylum problem* particular urgency is the growing scale of the abuse of the system ... By abusing [asylum], people from abroad with no legitimate claim to be here can fend off removal and secure a prolonged stay, during which they can work in the black economy and take advantage of a range of public services and benefits.
>
> (Anne Widdecombe cited in Young, C. 1997, 64).

What the reaction to refugees, asylum seekers and immigrants in general reveals is the way of thinking and acting that Malkki calls 'sedentarist' – a view of the world that values roots, place and order over mobility and fluidity. This leads us to think of mobile people as disruptive and morally suspicious. Place thus plays many roles in the construction of the refugee. At a metaphysical level it leads to suspicion of the mobile. At a legal level it makes the definition of the refugee possible. As a matter of history the construction of places called nations made the existence of the refugee as foreigner a possibility in the first place.

Conclusions

In this chapter we have explored some of the many ways in which conceptions of place are used in research. Being informed by place involves far more than simply writing about this place or that place. It involves thinking about the implications of the idea of place for whatever it is that is being researched – the construction of memory or the world of the homeless for instance. By looking at research on the creation of place in a mobile world, places of memory and places to live it becomes clear that place itself has a unique and pervasive power. There is no doubt that these acts of place-creation are political and contested and researching this 'politics of place' is an important strand of geographical enquiry. But the very fact that place is such a crucial site of contestation points toward its fundamental role in human life – the fact that we are placed beings. The basic unavoidability of place in human life makes it a very important object of politics. As we saw in Chapter 2, places may be socially constructed but they are necessary social constructions.

In the second half of this chapter we examined the role of place in the constitution of the normal and the 'pathological' – the 'in-place' and the 'out-of-place'. We saw how various conceptions of place and place as home played an active role in the constitution of the normal, the natural and the appropriate and how deviation from the expected relationship between place and practice led to labels of abnormality and inappropriateness. Here place is used to construct the taken-for-granted world. The homeless are not simply people without a roof over the head but people who are evaluated as being in the wrong place (the city, the country, outside, in public). Refugees are not simply people who are moving to escape persecution but people who are constituted by their displacement. Gays, lesbians and bisexuals are seen as 'out-of-place' because they disturb the heteronormative character of many of the places that surround us.

Writing about and researching place involves a multi-faceted understanding of the coming together of the physical world (both 'natural' and 'cultural'), the processes of meaning production and the practices of power that mark relations between social groups. The production of meaningful worlds in contexts of asymmetrical power relations occurs at all scales across the globe – from putting a poster on the wall to declaring a new nation. Places are produced by the people that constitute 'society' but at the same time they are key to the production of relations between people. Place, in other words, is right at the center of humanity.

Place appears in one form or another in the majority of research in human geography. It is easy to take this for granted as many of us entered geography as students thinking of it as being about places – places around the world. What this book has shown is that when reading research in human geography it is important to analyse how the writer is using place as a way of looking at the world. We have also seen how 'place' is not just a conceptual tool of geographers. It appears daily in our newspapers, in the pronouncements of politicians and in the social world that surrounds us. The furniture store tells us we can turn space into place; the real estate business tells us what kind of place we should want to live in; politicians and newspaper editors tell us that certain people are 'out-of-place'. Artists and writers attempt to evoke place in their work and architects try to literally create a sense of place in their buildings. 'Place', then, is not the sole property of human geographers. We are, however, in a unique position to both examine our own use of the concept and to cast a critical eye on the many ways place appears as a concept in everyday life. This can only add to the common-sense way in which geography is about places.

5

Place Resources

When it comes to place, life is fieldwork. The world itself is the best kind of resource for thinking about place. An observant geographer can learn a lot about place by reflecting on their everyday experience. Notice how, in Chapter 3, Doreen Massey develops her approach to place by walking down her local high street. Similarly David Harvey reflects on the newspaper accounts of a local area that he may have read over breakfast. Place not only surrounds us but is a key ingredient in many of the media through which we indirectly experience the world – the newspaper, film, music and literature. This chapter, however, focuses on more specialized resources for work on place. The most obvious resource, of course, is the literature on place from within geography and allied disciplines. This chapter introduces the key texts. In addition it indicates some useful web resources and suggests some projects on place.

Key Books on Place

The literature that uses place is endless. The following is a list of some of the key books (single authored and edited) that have taken place as a central concept. Many of them have been mentioned in this book.

Adams, Paul, Steven Hoelscher and Karen Till eds, 2001 *Textures of Place: Exploring Humanist Geographies* (Minneapolis, University of Minnesota Press).

A recent re-exploration of the humanistic approach of place and other geographical themes. The book was edited in honour of Yi-Fu Tuan and contains a wide range of essays by those students who have worked with him. A notable feature of the book is the way geographers and others informed by humanism have taken on board and developed the critiques of radical geographers without completely giving up on humanistic themes and insights.

Agnew, John 1987 *Place and Politics* (Boston, Allen and Unwin).

Agnew's book provides one of the clearest accounts of what place is and the role it plays in the development of formal politics. His three-part definition of place as location, locale and sense of place is widely used.

Agnew, John and James Duncan, eds. 1990 *The Power of Place* (Boston, Unwin Hyman).

An early example of work on place that is informed by the critical stance of the new cultural geography. The essays in this book take the concept of place, as developed in the 1970s and 1980s and reflect on the role place plays in the constitution of power and vice versa.

Anderson, Kay., and Faye Gale, eds. 1992 *Inventing Places: Studies in Cultural Geography* (London, Belhaven Press).

A collection of clearly written empirically rich accounts of the interrelations of place, power and representation – all informed by the theoretical traditions of the new cultural geography. One of the most accessible books for students.

Augé, Marc 1995 *Non-Places: Introduction to an Anthropology of Supermodernity* (London, Verso).

A widely read essay on the way in which old ideas of places as deeply rooted, authentic centers of meaning have been challenged by the increasing proliferation of places of movement and travel. Written from the perspective of a French anthropologist.

Buttimer, Anne and David Seamon, eds. 1980 *The Human Experience of Space and Place* (London, Croom Helm).

A collection of essays largely from the tradition of humanistic geography informed by phenomenology and existentialism. The essays focus on human experience, subjectivity and the nature of 'being-in-the-world'.

Casey, Edward 1993 *Getting Back Into Place: Toward a Renewed Understanding of the Place-World* (Bloomington IN, Indiana University Press).

Casey, Edward 1998 *The Fate of Place: A Philosophical History* (Berkeley, University of California Press).

These two books by the philosopher Edward Casey seek to understand why place has been relatively neglected by philosophers. The books consider the different ways in which philosophers have thought about or ignored place in their work and makes a carefully argued case for the importance of place. The earlier book is the more accessible.

Cresswell, Tim 1996 *In Place/Out of Place: Geography, Ideology and Transgression* (Minneapolis, University of Minnesota Press).

This book, informed by critical cultural theory, considers the role of place in constructing accepted ideas about what is appropriate and inappropriate. The focus is on acts of transgression where people are perceived to be acting 'out of place' and includes three extended case studies and a number of shorter stories about the role of place in the constitution of 'normality'.

Duncan, James and David Ley, eds. 1993 *Place/Culture/Representation* (New York, Routledge).

A collection of essays edited by geographers with backgrounds in both humanistic and critical approaches to geography which represent the new cultural geography approach to place and other geographical themes. The focus is very much on issues of representations of place.

Entrikin, Nicholas 1991 *The Betweenness of Place: Towards a Geography of Modernity* (London, Macmillan).

A rich and complicated book that develops the humanistic engagement with place into the 1990s. Entrikin argues that place is a realm that lies between the personal/subjective and the scientific/ objective worlds and thus needs to be understood in terms of what he calls narrative. Narratives (stories) are both shared and subjective and are thus well matched to the nature of place.

Hayden, Dolores 1995 *The Power of Place: Urban Landscapes as Public History* (Cambridge MA, MIT Press).

A very accessible and suggestive account of the role that place plays in the production of history, heritage and memory in a number of urban landscapes.

Jackson, Peter and Jan Penrose, eds. 1993 *Constructions of Race, Place, and Nation* (London, University College London Press).

A collection of essays that consider how places have been ideologically linked to notions of race. The authors show how both place and race are socio-cultural constructs that constantly refer to each other. This is clearest in the idea of a nation as a place with a particular racial identity.

Kearns, Gerard and Chris Philo eds. 1993 *Selling Places: the City as Cultural Capital, Past and Present* (Oxford, Pergamon).

An excellent, diverse collection of essays on how cities employ various kinds of representational strategies to promote their place above and beyond others with whom they compete. An important topic in a globalizing world where places battle each other for employment, cultural kudos and residents.

Lefebvre, Henri 1991 *The Production of Space* (Oxford: Blackwell).

Henri Lefebvre was a French urban and social theorist. His work has been very influential in radical human geography. Although 'place' is not the explicit concern here, his focus on 'social space' is very similar to the use of the term 'place' by human geographers. A central focus of this book is the creation of meanings for and in space in the context of a capitalist society.

Lippard, Lucy 1997 *The Lure of the Local: Senses of Place in a Multicentred Society* (New York, New Press).

Lippard, an artist and writer, considers how the idea of local places continues to be so necessary and appealing, even in a globalized and heterogeneous world. This accessible book provides an interesting counterpoint of the work of Augé and Meyrowitz on the idea of non-place.

Malpas, J E 1999 *Place and Experience: A Philosophical Topography* (Cambridge, Cambridge University Press).

A rich and complicated attempt by a philosopher to locate place at the center of considerations of human experience. He argues (like Casey and Sack) that place is a necessary bedrock for the constitution of society and culture.

Massey, Doreen 1994 *Space, Place and Gender* (Minneapolis, University of Minnesota Press).

This collection of essays by Doreen Massey includes important statements on ideas of place and home from a feminist perspective. It includes the important essay 'A Global Sense of Place' which is discussed in Chapter 3 of this book.

Meyrowitz, Joshua 1985 *No Sense of Place: The Impact of Electronic Media on Social Behaviour* (Oxford, Oxford University Press).

Meyrowitz argues that electronic media (particularly television) are producing an increasingly placeless world where experience is constantly mediated and homogenized. Should be read alongside Augé and Relph.

Nast, Heidi and Steve Pile, eds. 1998 *Places Through the Body* (London & New York, Routledge).

The 1990s saw a renewed interest in the body within human geography as well as in the wider world of social and cultural theory. The essays in this book examine the links between the body and place in a way which reinvigorates some of the work carried out by David Seamon twenty years earlier.

Relph, Edward 1976 *Place and Placelessness* (London, Pion).

One of the classic humanistic accounts of place in which Relph builds on the insights of Martin Heidegger to link the idea of place to the notion of 'authenticity'. He argues that modern landscapes are increasingly 'placeless' as they do not allow people to become 'existential insiders'. A pre-cursor to the work of Marc Augé.

Sack, Robert 1992 *Place, Consumption and Modernity* (Baltimore, Johns Hopkins University Press).

Sack, Robert 1997 *Homo Geographicus* (Baltimore, Johns Hopkins University Press).

Robert Sack's books have sought to place geography, and particularly the idea of place, at the center of our understanding of what it is to be in the world. In many ways these books build on the insights of humanistic geography. The first book considers the way place in the modern world is experienced through the processes of consumption while the second is an ambitious attempt to outline the primal significance of place to our understanding of morality and ethics. Should be read alongside Entrikin, Casey and Malpas.

Seamon, David 1979 *Geography of the Lifeworld: Movement, Rest, and Encounter* (New York, St. Martin's Press).

David Seamon's work is, like that of Relph and Tuan, based on the philosophy of phenomenology but differs from them in that Maurice Merleau-Ponty is the main inspiration. Thus Seamon's approach to place is far more focused on the body and everyday activities of the body than it is on understandings of rootedness and authenticity.

Shields, Robert 1991 *Places on the Margin* (London, Routledge).

Places on the Margin considers, through the development of British and North American case studies, the idea that places considered to be marginal are often symbolically central to the constitution of accepted forms of identity. Thus Brighton, a place of carnivalesque abandon, allows, through its licensing of unusual behavior, normal life to continue. This book is heavily influenced by Henri Lefebrvre and shares much with my *In Place/Out of Place*.

Tuan Yi-Fu 1974 *Topophilia: A Study of Environmental Perception, Attitudes and Values* (Englewood Cliffs, NJ, Prentice Hall).

Tuan Yi-Fu 1977 *Space and Place: The Perspective of Experience* (Minneapolis, University of Minnesota Press).

Tuan's work is central to any understanding of the idea of place in human geography and beyond. He has written many books on the subject but these two are the most widely cited. In them he develops the insight that the perceptions and values of human beings are central aspects of the human relation to the world and therefore need to be taken seriously. Place is the central concept which most perfectly expresses how humans create centers of meaning and fields of care in order to feel at home in the world.

Key Papers on Place

The following are important papers which tackle the difficult subject of theorizing place in a number of different contexts. The list is only suggestive of the wealth of literature on this subject.

Buttimer, Anne 1980 Home, Reach, and the Sense of Place, in *The Human Experience of Space and Place* Anne Buttimer and David Seamon, eds. (NY, St. Martins Press) 166–186.

Casey, Edward 1996 How to Get From Space to Place in a Fairly Short Stretch of Time: Phenomenological Prolegomena, in *Senses of Place* Steven Feld and Keith H. Basso, eds. (Santa Fe NM, School of American Research Press).

Cresswell, Tim 2002 Theorising Place in *Mobilizing Place, Placing Mobility* Tim Cresswell and Ginette Verstraete, eds. (Amsterdam, Rodopi) 11–32.

Curry, Michael R. 2002 Discursive Displacement and the Seminal Ambiguity of Space and Place, in *The Handbook of New Media: Social Shaping and Consequences of ICT* Leah Lievrouw and Sonia Livingstone, eds. (London, Sage Publications) 502–517.

Entrikin, J. Nicholas 2001 Hiding Places *Annals of the Association of American Geographers* 91:4, 694–697.

Entrikin, J. Nicholas 1989 Place, Region, and Modernity. in *The Power of Place* John Agnew and James S. Duncan, eds. (London, Unwin Hyman) 30–43.

Harvey, David 1993 From Space to Place and Back Again, in *Mapping the Futures: Local Cultures, Global Change* Jon Bird, Barry Curtis, Tim Putnam, George Robertson and Lisa Tickner, eds. (London, Routledge) 3–29. Also chapter 11 in David Harvey 1996 *Justice Nature and the Politics of Difference* (Oxford, Blackwell).

Lukerman, Fred 1964 Geography as a Formal Intellectual Discipline and the Way in Which it Contributes to Human Knowledge *Canadian Geographer* 8:4, 167–172.

Massey, Doreen 1993 Power-Geography and Progressive Sense of Place in *Mapping the Futures: Local Cultures, Global Change* Jon Bird, Barry Curtis, Tim Putnam, George Robertson and Lisa Tickner, eds. (London, Routledge) 59–69.

Massey, Doreen 1997 A Global Sense of Place in *Reading Human Geography* Trevor Barnes and Derek Gregory, eds. (London, Arnold) 315–323.

Merrifield, Andrew 1991 Place and Space: A Lefebvrian Reconciliation *Transactions of the Institute of British Geographers* 16:2: 516–531.

Oakes, Tim 1997 Place and the Paradox of Modernity *Annals of the Association of American Geographers* 87:3: 509–531.

Pred, Allan 1984 'Place as Historically Contingent Process: Structuration and the Time-Geography of Becoming Places' *Annals of the Association of American Geographers* 74:2, 279–297.

Rose, Gillian 1994 The Cultural Politics of Place: Local Representation and Oppositional Discourse in Two Films *Transactions of the Institute of British Geographers* 19: 46—60.

Seamon, David 1980 Body-Subject, Time-Space Routines and Place-Ballets, in *The Human Experience of Space and Place* Anne Buttimer and David Seamon, eds. (London, Croom Helm) 148–165.

Thrift, Nigel 1999 Steps to an Ecology of Place, in *Human Geography Today* Doreen Massey, John Allen and Philip Sarre, eds. (Cambridge, Polity Press) 295–322.

Tuan, Yi-Fu 1974 'Space and Place: Humanistic Perspective' *Progress in Human Geography* 6: 211–252.

Tuan, Yi-Fu 1991 Language and the Making of Place: A Narrative-Descriptive Approach' *Annals of the Association of American Geographers* 81:4, 684–696.

Tuan, Yi-Fu 1991 A View of Geography *Geographical Review* 81:1, 99–107.

Zukin, Sharon 1993 Market, Place and Landscape in *Landscapes of Power: From Detroit to Disney World* (Berkeley, University of California Press) 3-25.

Introductory Texts on Place

The following are books and papers on place that seek to introduce them in an accessible manner to students at all levels.

Bradford, Michael 2000 Geography: Pride of Place *Geography* 85:4, 311–321.

Cresswell, Tim 1999 Place, in *Introducing Human Geographies* Paul Cloke, Philip, Crang and Mark Goodwin, eds. (London, Arnold) 226–234.

Daniels, Stephen 1992 Place and the Geographical Imagination *Geography* 77: 310–322.

Holloway, Lewis and Phil Hubbard 2000 *People and Place: The Extraordinary Geographies of Everyday Life* (Upper Saddle River NJ, Prentice Hall).

McDowell, Linda 1997 ed. *Undoing Place? A Geographical Reader* (London, Edward Arnold).

Rose, Gillian 1995 Place and Identity: A Sense of Place, in *A Place in the World? Places, Cultures and Globalisation* Doreen Massey and Pat Jess eds. (Oxford, The Open University Press) 87–118.

Other Books and Papers on Place

The papers and books listed below are arranged thematically in groups. Rather than being about place per se they use the idea of place to examine other themes such as sport, the media or cyperspace.

Place, representation and popular culture

These books and paper focus on the way in which place is represented in the media, in film and in music.

Aitken, Stuart C. and Leo E. Zonn, eds. 1994 *Place, Power, Situation, and Spectacle : A Geography of Film* (Lanham, Md., Rowman & Littlefield).

Burgess, Jacquie and John Gold, eds. 1985 *Geography, the Media and Popular Culture* (London, Croom Helm).

Cresswell, Tim and Deborah Dixon, eds. 2002 *Engaging Film: Geographies of Mobility and Identity* (Lanham, Md., Rowman and Littlefield).

Curry, Michael 1998 *Digital Places: Living with Geographic Information Technologies.* (New York, Routledge).

Leyshon, Andrew; David Matless and George Revill, eds. 1998 *The Place of Music* (New York, Guilford).

Morley, David. 2001 Belongings: Place, Space and Identity in a Mediated World. *European Journal of Cultural Studies* 4:4, 425–448.

Zonn, Leo, ed. 1990 *Place Images in Media: Portrayal, Experience, and Meaning.* (Savage, MD, Rowman & Littlefield).

Place, exclusion and transgression

The following are books and papers that consider the role of place in the labeling of some people and practices as 'out-of-place' including women, the homeless, disabled people, gays, lesbians and bisexuals and other groups labeled as 'other' within western societies.

Boyer, Kate 1998 Place and the politics of virtue: clerical work, corporate anxiety, and changing meanings of public womanhood in early twentieth-century Montreal *Gender, Place and Culture: A Journal of Feminist Geography* 5:3, 261–275.

Brown, Michael P 2000 *Closet Space: Geographies of Metaphor from the Body to the Globe* (London, Routledge).

Cloke, Paul, Paul Milbourne & Rebekah Widdowfield 2000 Homelessness and Rurality: 'Out-of-Place' in Purified Space? *Environment and Planning D: Society & Space* 18:6, 715–735.

Domosh, Mona 1998 Geography and Gender: Home, Again? *Progress in Human Geography* 22:2, 276–282.

Duncan, Nancy, ed. 1996 *BodySpace: Destablizing Geographies of Gender and Sexuality.* (London, Routledge).

Forest, Benjamin 1995 West Hollywood as Symbol: The Significance of Place in the Construction of a Gay Identity *Environment and Planning D: Society and Space* 13:2, 133–157.

Halfacree, Keith 1996 'Out of Place in the Country: Travelers and the "Rural Idyll" '. *Antipode* 28:1, 42–72.

hooks, bell 1990 Homeplace: A Site of Resistance, *Yearning: Race, Gender, and Cultural Politics* (Boston, South End Press).

Kitchin, Rob M 1998 'Out of Place', Knowing One's Place: Towards a Spatialised Theory of Disability and Social Exclusion *Disability and Society* 13:3, 343–356.

May, Jon 2000 Of Nomads and Vagrants: Single Homelessness and Narratives of Home as Place *Environment and Planning D: Society and Space* 18:6, 737–759.

Pile, Steve and Michael Keith eds. 1997 *Geographies of Resistance* (London, Routledge).

Philo, Chris 1995 Animals, Geography, and the City: Notes on Inclusions and Exclusions *Environment and Planning D: Society and Space* 13:6, 655–681.

Radner, Hilary 1999 Roaming the City: Proper Women in Improper Places, in *Spaces of Culture: City – Nation – World* Mike Featherstone and Scott Lash, eds. (London, Sage Publications) 86–100.

Sibley, David 1995 *Geographies of Exclusion: Society and Difference in the West* (London, Routledge).

Valentine, Gill 1996 'Children Should be Seen and Not Heard: The Production and Transgression of Adult's Public Space' *Urban Geography* 17:3, 205–520.

Place and Sport

Place plays an important role in sport and leisure. Geographer John Bale has developed these links in several important books and papers.

Bale, John 1988 The Place of 'Place' in Cultural Studies of Sports *Progress in Human Geography* 12:4, 507–524.

Bale, John 1992 *Sport, Space, and the City* (London, Blackburn Press).

Other Approaches to Place: Ecology, Planning, Architecture

The principle focus of this book is the use of place within human geography. There are, however, other fields in which place has been a significant concept. One of these is the field of ecology and environmental ethics where places have been conceived of as tight connections between regions and their resources, flora and fauna. The principle conceptual term used in ecological approaches to place is 'bioregion.' Bioregions are:

> geographic areas having common characteristics of soil, watershed, climate, native plants and animals that exist within the whole planetary biosphere as unique and intrinsic contributive parts. A bioregion refers both to geographical terrain and a terrain of consciousness – to a place and the ideas that have developed about how to live in that place. A bioregion can be determined initially by use of climatology, physiography, animal and plant geography, natural history and other descriptive natural sciences. The final boundaries of a bioregion, however, are best described by the people who have lived within it, through human recognition of the realities of living-in-place. There is a distinctive resonance among living things and the factors that influence them which occurs specifically within each separate place on the planet. Discovering and describing that resonance is a way to describe a bioregion.
>
> Peter Berg, Director of the Plant Drum Foundation, and Raymond Dasmann, wildlife ecologist (cited at *http://home.klis.com/~chebogue/ p.amBio.html* (accessed 30 July 2003)).

Bioregionalists argue that our present system of places is arbitrary and too much the product of human artifice. They suggest that the present arrangement of political places disturbs the system of bioregions and makes it more difficult to solve ecological problems. Kirkpatrick Sale, in his book *Dwellers in the Land* makes the case for bioregional organisation in terms of scale, economy, polity and society. People, he argues, need to be close to their forms of government and life should be conducted on a scale where the effects of actions are clear and tanglible. Most human geographers would contend that his vision of place is far too restricted to the local and highly exclusionary. They would also suggest that the apparent naturalness of bioregions – often based on watertables – is in fact socially arbirtrary.

The following will provide a taste of this literature.

Berry, Wendell 1996 *The Unsettling of America* (San Francisco, Sierra Club Books).

Berthold-Bond, Daniel 2000 The Ethics of 'Place': Reflections on Bioregionalism. *Environmental Ethics* 22:1, 5–24.

Jackson, Wes 1994 *Becoming Native to This Place* (Lexington, University Press of Kentucky).

Norton, B.G., and B. Hannon 1997 Environmental Values: a Place-Based Theory. *Environmental Ethics* 19:3, 227–245.

Norton, Bryan and Bruce Hannon 1999 Democracy and Sense of Place Values in Environmental Policy, in *Philosophies of Place: Philosophy and Geography III* Andrew Light and Jonathan Smith, eds. (Lanham, Rowman and Littlefield).

Sale, Kirkpatrick 1985 *Dwellers in the Land: The Bioregional Vision* (San Francisco, Sierra Club).

Smith, Mick 2001 *An Ethics of Place: Radical Ecology, Postmodernity, and Social Theory.* (Albany, SUNY Press).

Snyder, Gary 1996 *A Place in Space: Ethics, Aesthetics and Watersheds* (San Francisco, Counterpoint Press).

Spretnak, Charlene 1997 *The Resurgence of the Real: Body, Nature, and Place in a Hypermodern World* (Reading, Mass., Addison-Wesley).

Wolch, Jennifer and Jody Emel eds. 1998 *Animal Geographies: Place, Politics, and Identity in the Nature-Culture Borderlands* (London, Verso).

Another tradition that frequently reflects on place is architecture and urban planning. These people, after all, are charged with the creation of material places. There have been many books written about the death of place as a result of architectural and planning processes. In addition there are the works of those such as Christopher Day and Christopher Alexander which seek to develop new ways of creating deeply felt places to produce a more rooted and meaningful life. There is much in common between the work of these architects and some forms of humanistic geography and they give a practical sense of the way ideas about place might be mobilized.

Alexander, Christopher 1977 *A Pattern Language: Towns, Buildings, Construction* (Oxford, Oxford University Press).

Arefi, Mahyar 1999 Non-Place and Placelessness as Narratives of Loss: Rethinking the Notion of Place *Journal of Urban Design* 4:2, 179–194.

Day, Christopher 1993 *Places of the Soul: Architecture and Design as a Healing Art* (London, Harper Collins).

Day, Christopher 2002 *Spirit and Place: Healing Our Environment* (London, Architectural Press).

Hiss, Tony 1990 *The Experience of Place* (New York, Knopf).

Kunstler, James 1994 *The Geography of Nowhere: The Rise and Decline of America's Manmade Landscape* (New York, Touchstone Books).

Lawrence, Denise L. and Setha M. Low 1990 The Built Environment and Spatial Form. *Annual Review of Anthropology* 19, 453–505.

Mugerauer, Robert 1994 *Interpretations on Behalf of Place* (Albany NY, State Univ. Press).

Norberg-Schulz, Christian 1980 *Genius Loci: Towards a Phenomenology of Architecture.* (New York, Rizzoli).

Walters, E V 1988 *Placeways: A Theory of the Human Environment* (Chapel Hill, University of North Carolina Press).

Key Journals

The most up to date writing on place can be found in specialist academic journals centered on the discipline of geography. Regularly checking some of these journals will enable you to see how the concept of place continues to evolve and how researchers and writers use the concept in different and often competing ways. The list is limited to journals printed in English.

The Transactions of the Institute of British Geographers
The Annals of the Association of American Geographers
Australian Geographer
Canadian Geographer
The New Zealand Geographer
Area
The Professional Geographer

These journals all cover the broad range of geography both human and physical and are often the main publication outlets for national geographical societies. They are considered leading places to publish work that speaks to international audiences.

Antipode: A Radical Journal of Geography

This journal focuses on work that links academic inquiry to social and political change and activism. Work is normally informed by radical theoretical traditions such as Marxism, feminism and anarchism.

Gender, Place and Culture

Papers here focus on the interrelations between gender, sexuality and geography. It is a major outlet of geographers informed by feminism.

Environment and Planning D: Society and Space

Papers in this journal tend to be a little more theoretically focused than in other journals. It is usually a place to find 'cutting-edge' developments in the field.

Progress in Human Geography

This is an excellent place to read reviews of geography's various subfields and papers which attempt to summarise developments in the field and suggest innovative ways forward.

Political Geography

This journal deals with the interactions between the geographical world (including place) and various levels of politics from the formal and institutional to the more everyday variety. A good place to look for work on boundaries, the nation, regional governance etc.

Journal of Historical Geography

A good place to find in-depth articles on places in the past as well as the role place plays in the construction of memory and heritage.

Cultural Geographies (formally Ecumene)
Social and Cultural Geography

These journals both focus on cultural/social geography and therefore include many papers on the construction, maintenance and transformation of meaning and practice in place.

Ethics, Place and Environment

Here papers focus on ethical issues within geography. These issues include environmental ethics and the role of place in the construction of 'moral geographies'.

Health and Place

The journal for medical geography which specializes in the inter-relations between geography and medical issues such as healthy and unhealthy places, contagion, historical beliefs about environmental impacts on health, etc.

Web Resources

There are, of course, endless websites about particular places – almost any place in the Western world has its own site. The sites listed here are more directly related to the concept of place and to those writers who are referred to in this book.

http://www.augustana.ca/~janzb/place/

This website, constructed by Bruce B. Janz, an Associate Professor of Philosophy at Augustana University College, Canada is a rich resource for scholars interested in place and space. He has pulled together tremendous amounts of material from a huge range of disciplines and made it available to people interested in these themes worldwide. It includes readings and websites as well as some interesting quotes and comments.

http://www.placematters.net/

Place Matters is based in New York City and is an organization devoted to preserving and promoting particular places within the city. It includes a census of places that matter to New Yorkers and a short account of why they think place matters.

http://www.cnr.berkeley.edu/community_forestry/Place_bib.htm

This is a working bibliography of place material from the University of California at Berkeley.

http://www.lclark.edu/~soan370/global/nomads.html

A fascinating site examining the role of place and non-place in a number of advertisements.

http://www.dareonline.org/themes/space/index.html

A site called 'space and place' which uses art and suggestive text to explore the relationships between space, place, boundaries and movement.

http://www.reaktionbooks.co.uk/list_topographics.html

A site promoting a series of books called 'topographics'. This is writing about place that combines academic approaches with personal reflection and creative writing.

http://www.cybergeo.presse.fr

A European multi-lingual cyber journal for geographers.

http://www.acme-journal.org

A cyber journal for critical geography.

http://www.headmap.org

A fascinating creative venture that considers issues of place, space and mapping in a cyberspace context.

A number of websites are dedicated to architectural and ecological views of place. These include:

http://home.klis.com/~chebogue/p.amBio.html

A website on bioregionalism

http://www.gutenbergdump.net/axe/placequiz.htm

A quiz which asks 'how well do you know your place?' Based on a bioregional perspective.

http://www.olywa.net/speech/may99/mccloskey.html

A paper by David McCloskey called 'A Bioregion is a Life-Place'.

http://www.webcom.com/penina/spirit-and-place/

This website briefly introduces the work of Christopher Day, a British architect who attempts to produce a 'spirit of place' in his architecture.

Student Projects and Exercises

Choosing a project for a term paper, honours thesis or dissertation is a difficult task. The best advice I have seen is in *Doing Cultural Geography* edited by Pamela Shurmer-Smith (2002). Here the authors remark that students often have an interest in a particular topic but cannot put their finger on what it is that makes the topic interesting. This leads to enthusiastic but fragmented term papers. Their suggestion is to start from a different perspective. Instead of starting with a topic they suggest starting with a perspective or theoretical approach and *then* finding a broad topic that will illustrate and bear the weight of that approach.

Most work on place, including the ideas for projects below, will be qualitative in nature. It is true that some forms of quantitative work might provide background information on place but the centrality of subjectivity and experience to the concept of place meant that documentary research, visual analysis, observation, interviewing and ethnographic forms of research will be the most prominent methodologies.

The following are very broad sets of suggestions of theoretical and empirical areas that produce good student projects. The list is in no way comprehensive. It is supposed to suggest the breadth of topics that geographers can study. They also overlap considerably.

Place and representation

How are places represented? Who has the power to represent? What is left un-represented? Why are places used in particular forms of representation?

The focus here could be on a place near you. Most towns and cities are represented in some way by local tourist offices, local government, estate agents (realtors) etc. Alternatively you could look at some form of artistic representation such as literature, film, music or the internet. Think, for instance, of the way Los Angeles features in Hollywood films, or the way the Australian outback plays a role in films such as *Priscilla: Queen of the Desert* and *Crocodile Dundee*. Alternatively you could think of the way particular places are associated with forms of representation. In popular music for instance we frequently hear of place sounds such as 'The Mersey Beat' (Liverpool), Cool Cymru (Wales) or Motown (Detroit).

Anachorism – being out of place

What role does place play in the constitution of 'normality'? How are particular activities, people and objects associated with particular places? Who decides that activities, people and objects are out of place (anachoristic)?

The local and national media are a good place to find examples of this. Recent examples in the UK include prostitution in rural areas, asylum seekers and post-modern tower blocks in Brighton and Hove. In the US there are on-going discussions on the role of immigration in the construction of American place as well as more specific accounts of the construction of particular forms of transnational place on the US-Mexico borderland. Internationally there has been discussion of Greece's first official mosque near Athens (in time for the Olympics), the presence of horses and ponies on housing projects in Dublin and the plight of gypsy travelers in Eastern Europe. Almost everywhere there is ongoing discussion of the 'place' of the homeless. Examples of anachorism are almost endless.

Global senses of place

How are traditional senses of place being altered by the process of globalisation? How does transnational trade operate through and in place? What effect does the Internet have on our relations to local place? How are virtual places created in cyberspace? How are global senses of place produced through food, music or clothing? Does increased mobility on a global scale produce placeless places?

Almost any place in the Western world includes people, objects and ideas from elsewhere. Look around you and you will see this. How is your local place (of residence, work or education) constructed from the outside by these flows? Perhaps you could choose one element of everyday life and explore its impact on your place. This could be world music, immigrant groups, 'ethnic' food or globalized forms of protests politics.

Place and memory

How is place linked to history? What memories are memorialized in the material landscape? What memories are hidden? How is memory contested?

As we have seen place is an important component in the construction of memory. Heritage areas and museums are sprouting up everywhere. Find a local museum that is supposed to represent the city of region in which you live and explore its representational strategies. How does it create a sense of place through connections to the past? How are areas of residence zoned through planning to reproduce particular ideas about the past? It is important when conducting these projects to consider the kinds of memories that are not being reproduced in these places. Why is this? Places are not just small-scale and local. Nations are places too. How are nations constructed in relation to selective histories? How, for instance, are the pasts of native peoples in North America, Australia or New Zealand marginalized or brought to the fore in discussions of the nation? How are the experiences and memories of the most recent immigrants excluded or included?

Practice and Place

How are practice and place connected? How does the repetition of everyday activities produce a particular sense of place? How are places constructed to encourage some forms of practice and discourage others?

It is necessary to get beyond consideration of the material form of places and representations of them in order to fully understand place. The things that people do can never be fully predicted and the best-laid plans are often transformed by the stubborn repetition of practice. How is your place practiced? What forms of repetition can be observed producing a unique kind of 'place-ballet'? How does a place change through the day? What are its rhythmic geographies? What kinds of practices disturb these repetitions? A lot of work on practice will be about the mundane practices of everyday life and this is sometimes difficult to write about and research because it is so unremarkable. Careful observation will be necessary for such projects.

Place and Politics

How do politicians promote places through the creation of political territory? What representational strategies are used to create political places from the local to the global? How do processes of internationalization on the one hand, and devolution on the other create a new landscape of places?

Place is important to politicians. Politicians from the local council to the United Nations want to encourage a sense of belonging and citizenship. In order to do this they have created communities of people that feel as though they 'belong' to a place. Since the eighteenth century, politicians have been creating the place of the nation through such strategies as the conferral of citizenship rights, national anthems, passports, creation myths and monumental spaces.

More recently regional politicians have sought to promote particular images of their region-as-place. In the UK, this has been prominent in places such as Wales and Scotland but also within England in the North or Cornwall for instance. In the US, states have consistently fought with the federal government over the allegiance of citizens. Texas is a good example of this. On another level some places in the US have been promoted as more liberal places to live by their local politicians – think of West Hollywood or Vermont. Finally politicians on an international scale have sought to produce places that subsume nations. The European Union is an obvious example.

Bibliography

Agnew J 1987 *The United States in the World Economy* Cambridge University Press, Cambridge.

Agnew J A 2002 *Place and Politics in Modern Italy* University of Chicago Press, Chicago, London.

Aitken S C and Zonn L eds. 1994 *Place, Power, Situation, and Spectacle: A Geography of Film* Rowman & Littlefield, Lanham, MD.

Anderson B R O G 1991 *Imagined Communities: Reflections on the Origin and Spread of Nationalism* Verso, London, New York.

Anderson K 1991 *Vancouver's Chinatown: Racial Discourse in Canada, 1875–1980* McGill-Queen's University Press, Montreal.

Anderson K 1996 Cultural Hegemony and the Race-Definition Process in Chinatown, Vancouver: 1880–1980 in Hamnett C, ed. *Social Geography: A Reader* Arnold, London 209–235.

Appleby S 1990 Crawley: A Space Mythology *New Formations* 11, 19–44.

Augé M 1995 *Non-Places: Introduction to an Anthropology of Supermodernity* Verso, London, New York.

Bachelard G 1994 *The Poetics of Space* Beacon Press, Boston.

Barnes T J and Gregory D eds.1997 *Reading Human Geography: The Poetics and Politics of Inquiry* Wiley, London, New York.

Bauman Z 1995 *Life in Fragments: Essays in Postmodern Morality* Blackwell, Oxford.

Bell D and Valentine G eds. 1995 *Mapping Desire: Geographies of Sexualities* Routledge, London, New York.

Bell D, Binnie J, Cream J and Valentine G 1994 All Hyped up and No Place to Go *Gender, Place and Culture* 1, 31–47.

Bird J, Curtis B, Robertson G and Tickner L eds. 1993 *Mapping the Futures: Local Cultures, Global Change* Routledge, London, New York.

Brown M P 2000 *Closet Space: Geographies of Metaphor from the Body to the Globe* Routledge, London, New York.

Burgess J A and Gold J R eds. 1985 *Geography, the Media & Popular Culture* Croom Helm, London.

Buttimer A 1971 *Society and Milieu in the French Geographic Tradition* Published for the Association of American Geographers by Rand McNally, Chicago.

Buttimer A and Seamon D eds. 1980 *The Human Experience of Space and Place* St. Martin's Press, New York.

Carrington D 1984 *Granite Island: A Portrait of Corsica* Penguin, London.

Casey E 1996 How to Get from Space to Place in a Fairly Short Stretch of Time in Feld, S. and Baso, K. eds. *Senses of Place* School of American Research, Santa Fe 14–51.

Casey E S 1987 *Remembering: A Phenomenological Study* Indiana University Press, Bloomington.

Casey E S 1998 *The Fate of Place: A Philosophical History* University of California Press, Berkeley.

Charlesworth A 1994 Contesting Places of Memory: The Case of Auschwitz *Environment and Planning D: Society and Space* 12:5, 579–593.

Christaller W and Baskin C W 1966 *Central Places in Southern Germany* Prentice-Hall, Englewood Cliffs, NJ.

Clayton D W 2000 *Islands of Truth: The Imperial Fashioning of Vancouver Island* UBC Press, Vancouver.

Cloke P, Milbourne P and Widdowfield R 2000 Homelessness and Rurality: 'Out-of-Place' in Purified Space? *Environment and Planning D: Society and Space* 18:6, 715–735.

Cosgrove D 1984 *Social Formation and Symbolic Landscape* Croom Helm, London.

Craddock S 2000 *City of Plagues: Disease, Poverty, and Deviance in San Francisco* University of Minnesota Press, Minneapolis.

Cresswell T 1994 Putting Women in Their Place: The Carnival at Greenham Common *Antipode* 26:1, 35–58.

Cresswell T 1996 *In Place/Out of Place: Geography, Ideology and Transgression* University of Minnesota Press, Minneapolis.

Cresswell T 2001 *The Tramp in America* Reaktion, London.

Cresswell T and Dixon D eds. 2002 *Engaging Film: Geographies of Mobility and Identity* Rowman & Littlefield, Lanham, MD.

Cronon W 1991 *Nature's Metropolis: Chicago and the Great West* Norton, New York.

Cronon W 1992 Kennecott Journey: The Paths out of Town in Cronon, W., Miles, G. and Gitlin, J. eds. *Under an Open Sky* Norton, New York 28–51.

de Certeau M 1984 *The Practice of Everyday Life* University of California Press, Berkeley, CA.

de Lauretis T 1990 Eccentric Subjects: Feminist Theory and Historical Consciousness *Feminist Studies* 16:1, 115–150.

Desforges L & Maddern J forthcoming Front Doors to Freedom, Portal to the Past: History at the Ellis Island Immigration Museum, New York *Journal of Social and Cultural Geography*.

Deutsche R 1988 Uneven Development: Public Art in New York City *October* 47, 3–52.

Douglas M 1966 *Purity and Danger; an Analysis of Concepts of Pollution and Taboo* Praeger, New York.

Duncan N 1996 Renegotiating Gender and Sexuality in Public and Private Spaces in Duncan, N. ed *Bodyspace* Routledge, London 127–45.

Edensor T 2002 *National Identity, Popular Culture and Everyday Life* Berg, Oxford, New York.

Entriken J N 1985 Humanism, Naturalism and Geographic Thought *Geographical Analysis* 17, 243–247.

Entriken J N 1991 *The Betweenness of Place: Towards a Geography of Modernity* Macmillan, London.

Escobar A 2001 Culture Sits in Places: Reflections on Globalism and Subaltern Strategies of Localization *Political Geography* 20:2, 139–74.

Fleure H 1919 (1996) Human Regions in Agnew, J., Livingstone, D. and Rogers, A. eds. *Human Geography: An Essential Anthology* Blackwell, Oxford 385–387.

Foote K E 1997 *Shadowed Ground: America's Landscapes of Violence and Tragedy* University of Texas Press, Austin.

Forest B 1995 West Hollywood as Symbol: The Significance of Place in the Construction of a Gay Identity *Environment and Planning D: Society and Space* 13:2, 133–157.

Gandy M 2002 *Concrete and Clay: Reworking Nature in New York City* MIT Press, Cambridge, MA.

Giordano B 2000 Italian Regionalism or "Padanian' Nationalism – the Political Project of the Lega Nord in Italian Politics *Political Geography* 19:41, 445–471.

Gregory D 1998 *Explorations in Critical Human Geography: Hettner-Lecture 1997* Department of Geography University of Heidelberg, Heidelberg.

Hartshorne R 1959 *Perspective on the Nature of Geography* Published for the Association of American Geographers by Rand McNally, Chicago.

Hartshorne R 1939 *The Nature of Geography; a Critical Survey of Current Thought in the Light of the Past* The Association, Lancaster, PA.

Harvey D 1989 *The Condition of Postmodernity*, Blackwell, Oxford.

Harvey D 1996 *Justice, Nature and the Geography of Difference* Blackwell Publishers, Cambridge, MA.

Harvey D 2000 *Spaces of Hope* University of California Press, Berkeley.

Hayden D 1995 *The Power of Place: Urban Landscapes as Public History* MIT Press, Cambridge, MA.

Hebdige D 1988 *Subculture: The Meaning of Style* Routledge, London.

Heidegger M 1971 *Poetry, Language, Thought* Harper & Row, New York.

Herbertson A 1905 The Major Natural Regions: An Essay in Systematic Geography *Geographical Journal* 25, 300–312.

hooks b 1990 *Yearning: Race, Gender, and Cultural Politics* South End Press, Boston, MA.

Hoskins G forthcoming A Place to Remember. Scaling the Walls of Angel Island Immigration Station *Journal of Historical Geography*.

Hubbard P 1997 Red-Light Districts and Toleration Zones: Geographies of Female Street Prostitution in England and Wales *Area* 29:2, 129–140.

Hubbard P 1998 Community Action and the Displacement of Street Prostitution: Evidence from British Cities *Geoforum* 29:3, 269–286.

Hubbard P 2000 Desire/Disgust: Mapping the Moral Contours of Heterosexuality *Progress in Human Geography* 24 191–217.

Jackson J B 1997 *Landscape in Sight: Looking at America* Yale University Press, New Haven, CT.

Jackson P 1989 *Maps of Meaning* Unwin Hyman, London.

Johnson N C 1994 Sculpting Heroic Histories: Celebrating the Centenary of the 1798 Rebellion in Ireland *Transactions of the Institute of British Geographers* 19:1, 78–93.

Johnson N C 1996 Where Geography and History Meet: Heritage Tourism and the Big House in Ireland *Annals of the Association of American Geographers* 86:3, 551–566.

Johnston R J 1991 *A Question of Place: Exploring the Practice of Human Geography* Blackwell, Oxford.

Kearns G and Philo C eds. 1993 *Selling Places: The City as Cultural Capital, Past and Present* Pergamon Press, Oxford, New York.

Kitchin R 1998 'Out of Place', 'Knowing One's Place': Space, Power and the Exclusion of Disabled People *Disability and Society* 13:3, 343–356.

Lefebvre H 1991 *The Production of Space* Blackwell, Oxford, UK.

Ley D 1977 Social Geography and the Taken-for-Granted World *Transactions of the Institute of British Geographers* 2:4, 498–512.

Leyshon A, Matless D and Revill G eds. 1998 *The Place of Music* Guilford Press, New York.

Lippard L 1997 *The Lure of the Local: Senses of Place in a Multicultural Society* The New Press, New York.

Lösch A 1954 *The Economics of Location* Yale University Press, New Haven, CT.

Lukerman F 1964 Geography as a Formal Intellectual Discipline and the Way in Which It Contributes to Human Knowledge *Canadian Geographer* 8:4, 167–172.

MacLeod G and Jones M 2001 Renewing the Geography of Regions *Environment and Planning D: Society and Space* 19:6, 669–695.

Malkki L 1992 National Geographic: The Rooting of Peoples and the Territorialization of National Identity among Scholars and Refugees *Cultural Anthropology* 7:1, 24–44.

Malpas J E 1999 *Place and Experience: A Philosophical Topography* Cambridge University Press, Cambridge.

Martin B and Mohanty C 1986 Feminist Politics: What's Home Got to Do with It? in de Lauretis, T. ed *Feminist Studies/Cultural Studies* Indiana University Press, Bloomington 191–212.

Massey D 1997 A Global Sense of Place in Barnes, T. and Gregory, D. eds. *Reading Human Geography* Arnold, London 315–323.

May J 1996 Globalization and the Politics of Place: Place and Identity in an Inner London Neighbourhood *Transactions of the Institute of British Geographers* 21:1, 194–215.

May J 2000 Of Nomads and Vagrants: Single Homelessness and Narratives of Home as Place *Environment and Planning D: Society and Space* 18:6, 737–759.

Meyrowitz J 1985 *No Sense of Place: The Impact of Electronic Media on Social Behavior* Oxford University Press, New York.

Newman O 1972 *Defensible Space* Macmillan, New York.

Paasi A 1996 *Territories, Boundaries, and Consciousness: The Changing Geographies of the Finnish-Russian Border* J. Wiley & Sons, Chichester.

Paasi A 2002 Place and Region: Regional Worlds and Words *Progress in Human Geography* 26:6, 802–811.

Parr H and Philo C 1995 Mapping Mad Identities in Pile, S. and Thrift, N. eds. *Mapping the Subject* Routledge, London 199–225.

Philo C 1987 'The Same and the Other': On Geographies, Madness and Outsiders Loughborough University of Technology Department of Geography Occasional Paper 11.

Philo C 1992 The Child in the City *Journal of Rural Studies* 8:2, 193–207.

Philo C 1995 Animals, Geography, and the City: Notes on Inclusions and Exclusions *Environment and Planning D: Society and Space* 13:6, 655–681.

Pratt G 1999 Geographies of Identity and Difference: Marking Boundaries in Massey, D., Allen, J. and Sarre, P. eds. *Human Geography Today* Polity, Cambridge 151–168.

Pred A R 1984 Place as Historically Contingent Process: Structuration and the Time-Geography of Becoming Places *Annals of the Association of American Geographers* 74:2, 279–297.

Raban J 1999 *Passage to Juneau: A Sea and Its Meanings* Pantheon Books, New York.

Reid L and Smith N 1993 John Wayne Meets Donald Trump: The Lower East Side as Wild Wild West in Kearns, G. and Philo, C. eds. *Selling Places: The City as Cultural Capital, Past and Present* Pergamon, Oxford 193–209.

Relph E 1976 *Place and Placelessness* Pion, London.

Rose G 1993 *Feminism and Geography: The Limits of Geographical Knowledge* Polity, Cambridge.

Sack R 1992 *Place, Consumption and Modernity* Johns Hopkins University Press, Baltimore.

Sack R 1997 *Homo Geographicus* Johns Hopkins University Press, Baltimore.

Sassen S 1999 *Guests and Aliens* New Press, New York.

Sauer C O and Leighly J 1963 *Land and Life; a Selection from the Writings of Carl Ortwin Sauer* University of California Press, Berkeley.

Seamon D 1979 *A Geography of the Lifeworld: Movement, Rest, and Encounter* St. Martin's Press, New York.

Seamon D 1980 Body-Subject, Time-Space Routines, and Place-Ballets in Buttimer, A. and Seamon, D. eds. *The Human Experience of Space and Place* Croom Helm, London 148–65.

Sibley D 1981 *Outsiders in Urban Societies* St. Martin's Press, New York.

Smith N 1991 *Uneven Development: Nature, Capital, and the Production of Space* B. Blackwell, Oxford.

Smith N 1996 *The New Urban Frontier: Gentrification and the Revanchist City* Routledge, London.

Soja E W 1989 *Postmodern Geographies: The Reassertion of Space in Critical Social Theory* Verso, London.

Soja E 1999 Thirdspace: Expanding the Scope of the Geographical Imagination in Massey, D., Allen, J. and Sarre, P. eds. *Human Geography Today* Polity, Cambridge 260–278.

Taylor P J 1999 *Modernities: A Geohistorical Interpretation* Polity Press, Cambridge.

Thrift N 1983 On the Determination of Social Action in Time and Space *Environment and Planning D: Society and Space* 1:1, 23–57.

Thrift N 1994 Inhuman Geographies: Landscapes of Speed, Light and Power in Cloke, P. Ed *Writing the Rural: Five Cultural Geographies* Paul Chapman, London 191–250.

Thrift N J 1996 *Spatial Formations* Sage, London, Thousand Oaks, CA.

Thrift N 1997 The Still Point: Resistance, Expressiveness Embodiment and Dance in Pile, S. and Keith, M. eds. *Geographies of Resistance* Routledge, London 124–151.

Till K 1993 Neotraditional Towns and Urban Villages: The Cultural Production of a Geography of 'Otherness' *Environment and Planning D: Society and Space* 11:6, 709–732.

Till K 1999 Staging the Past: Landscape Designs, Cultural Identity, and Erinnerungspolitik at Berlin's Neue Wache, *Ecumene* 6:3, 251–283.

Tuan Yi-Fu 1974a Space and Place: Humanistic Perspective *Progress in Human Geography* 6, 211–252.

Tuan Yi-Fu 1974b *Topophilia: A Study of Environmental Perception, Attitudes, and Values* Prentice-Hall, Englewood Cliffs, NJ.

Tuan Yi-Fu 1977 *Space and Place: The Perspective of Experience* University of Minnesota Press, Minneapolis.

Tuan Yi-Fu 1991a Language and the Making of Place: A Narrative-Descriptive Approach *Annals of the Association of American Geographers* 81:4, 684–696.

Tuan Yi-Fu 1991b A View of Geography *Geographical Review* 81:1, 99–107.

Tuitt P 1996 *False Images: Law's Construction of the Refugee* Pluto Press, London.

Valentine G 1993 (Hetero)Sexing Space: Lesbian Perspectives and Experiences of Everyday Spaces. *Environment and Planning D: Society and Space* 11:4, 395–413.

Valentine G 1997 Angels and Devils: Moral Landscapes of Childhood *Environment and Planning D: Society and Space* 14:5, 581–599.

Veness A 1992 Home and Homelessness in the United States; Changing Ideals and Realities *Environment and Planning D: Society and Space* 10:4, 445–468.

Wagner P L and Mikesell M W eds. 1962 *Readings in Cultural Geography* University of Chicago Press, Chicago.

White A 2002 Geographies of Asylum, Legal Knowledge Andd Legal Practices *Political Geography* 21:8, 1055–1073.

Williams R 1960 *Border Country* Chatto and Windus, London.

Williams R 1985 *Keywords: A Vocabulary of Culture and Society* Oxford University Press, New York.

Young C 1997 Political Representation of Geography and Place in the United Kingdom Asylum and Immigration Bill (1995) *Urban Geography* 18:1, 62–73.

Young I M 1997b *Intersecting Voices: Dilemmas of Gender, Political Philosophy, and Policy* Princeton University Press, Princeton, NJ.

Index